The UK Economy 1999-2009

Ian Black

Head of Economics, St. Albans School

anforme

© Anforme Ltd 2010
ISBN 978-1-905504-35-0

Anforme Ltd, Stocksfield Hall, Stocksfield, Northumberland NE43 7TN.

Typeset by George Wishart & Associates, Whitley Bay.
Printed by Potts, Cramlington.

Contents

Introduction

Macroeconomics has always been a subject that is constantly changing. The reason why it is so fun to learn and teach is that it is usually very easy to discover fresh insights on, and examples of, traditional economic theories and concepts. However, the events of the past two and a half years have been tumultuous even by the standards of the UK economy. It seems strange to think that just three years ago economists were talking about the disappearance of the business cycle, Western governments' finances were seemingly under control, and nobody outside of Japan had ever heard of quantitative easing. Given all of the changes in the world of Economics, a third edition of 'The UK Economy' became both tempting and necessary in equal measure.

Those familiar with the first two editions of 'The UK Economy' will find this new edition a little different. KS5 qualifications in Economics, as with most academic qualifications, have become less knowledge-based and increasingly skills-based: a trend that has persisted for at least the eleven years that I have been teaching. In the main, I have tried to shrink the content of the book down to the essential concepts that pupils will need to know for A level, IB and Pre U.

The four main skills that pupils are required to demonstrate are (i) Knowledge and Understanding, (ii) Application, (iii) Analysis and (iv) Evaluation. Each section of each chapter in the book therefore contains one of these headings, under which I have attempted to demonstrate the appropriate skill. (Occasionally, there may be some overlap so as not to disturb the narrative flow.) There is also 'Extension Material' for gifted and talented pupils and indeed any other interested readers, which others may choose to skip. The questions could be used in class to test pupil understanding or as homework exercises. Sometimes, clues to the answers can be found by reading the appropriate chapter. At other times, I have deliberately not included the relevant material in order to invite pupils to research the answers themselves and do their own thinking.

Many thanks to Peter Maunder, Tracey Peek and my 6th form pupils at St Albans School for all of their helpful comments and suggestions on how to improve this book. Any 'deliberate' mistakes that remain are entirely my own.

Ian Black
January 2010

Chapter 1

GDP – From Boom to Bust!

published in 2009, no 1999-2009

In this Chapter we first review the growth performance of the UK economy during the past ten years. Reasons why the economy went into recession in 2008 are then itemised. The Chapter then considers the constituent items of GDP making clear the dependence on consumer spending in driving the UK's recent economic growth. The Chapter concludes in considering reasons for the sluggish growth in manufacturing compared with the growth of the service sector.

● Knowledge: Economic growth

Economic growth is defined as a rise in the productive potential of the economy over a period of time. Because of the practical impossibilities of using productive potential as a measure of growth, economists use a **proxy variable**. The most commonly used is Gross Domestic Product or **GDP**.

One of the government's four key macroeconomic objectives is to achieve stable, positive economic growth. However, there has been no formal GDP growth plan or target since the 1960s. Today, the cornerstone of UK macroeconomic policy is the **inflation target**, set by the government and delivered by the Bank of England. This is partly because price stability is a necessary condition for stable economic growth, so price stability is a means to an end as well as an end in itself. The Bank of England's mandate includes "support(ing) the Government's economic policy, including its objectives for growth and employment".[1] Economic growth is of critical importance due to the positive relationship between growth and living standards.

● Application: The growth performance

Figure 1.1: UK annual real GDP growth, 1998-2008

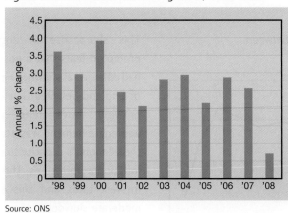

Source: ONS

Figure 1.1 shows recent trends in UK annual real GDP growth. The remarkable thing about GDP growth until 2008 was its stability, especially when compared to the turbulent times of the 1970s, 1980s and early 1990s. The Labour government had pledged to reduce the fluctuations in the business cycle. Until 2008, it looked like it had succeeded. By the first quarter of 2008, GDP had expanded for no less than 63 consecutive quarters. However, GDP contracted in the second and third quarter of 2008 as shown in Figure 1.2. **Recession** is defined as two successive negative quarters of real GDP growth. Thus by the third quarter of 2008 the economy was then in recession.

Question

1. Describe what happened to the level of real GDP between 2004 and 2005.

---

1. Letter from the Chancellor to the Governor, 6 May 1997, in *Bank of England Quarterly Bulletin*, August 1997.

Figure 1.2: The UK business cycle: quarterly data

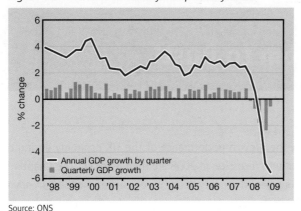

Source: ONS

When the Labour government came to power in 1997 it revised the estimated trend growth rate downwards from 2.5% to 2.25%. In 1999 it revised the figure back up to 2.5% and in 2002 it was further revised upwards to 2.75%. Average real GDP growth was a healthy 2.8% between 1995 and 2008, which provides strong evidence that this upward revision was justified.

The output gap is actual output minus trend output as a percentage of trend output. Data for 2008/9 is a forecast.

● Analysis: Explaining fluctuations in real GDP growth

1998-2000: A Mini-Boom

A mini-boom in the UK took place despite the Asian financial crisis of 1998. The mini-boom was largely due to high growth of consumer spending, in turn due to:

- Relatively low interest rates.
- Rising real incomes.
- The gain in household wealth arising from higher house prices and building society windfalls.

The Bank of England base rate fell from 7.25% in May 1998 to 5% by June 1999, encouraging consumers to spend, either by running down their savings or by borrowing. The large rise in house prices that year led to a **wealth effect**: as consumers get wealthier, they tend to spend more. This may be simply because they feel wealthier, or it may be because they have borrowed more money secured on the rising value of their properties (see Chapter 2). The elusive 'feel-good factor', missing for many years in the 1990s, finally appeared to have returned to the UK economy. Between 1997 and 2004, real consumer expenditure grew by 3.7% on average, compared to 1.1% between 1990 and 1995. This sharp upturn in consumer spending was followed in 1998 by a 14% rise in **investment**, indicating evidence of an **accelerator effect** for the UK economy.

Figure 1.3: The UK output gap between 1997/8 and 2009/10

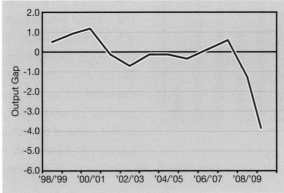

Source: HM Treasury

This sharp rise in aggregate demand prompted fears that a positive **output gap** had emerged as shown in Figure 1.3. The Bank of England believed that the economy was growing above trend: in other words, aggregate demand was accelerating beyond the economy's capacity to supply, leading to inflationary pressures. The Bank duly raised interest rates and this contributed to a moderate slowdown of economic growth as shown in Figure 1.3.

2001-2002: Slowdown

The sharp decline in global growth, particularly in the US, the UK's biggest trading partner, largely accounted for the slowdown, and in the final quarter of 2001 UK growth was reported at 0%, although it was subsequently revised upwards. The manufacturing sector was the biggest sufferer and in the year to

Consumer spending has helped to support growth in the economy.

November 2001 manufacturing output fell by 5.4%, its biggest fall since 1991. Nonetheless, the economy as a whole grew by almost 2.5% in 2001, a quicker rate than all of its G7 competitors for the first time in fifteen years.

The tragic events of 11 September 2001 (9/11) led to a sharp fall in UK business and consumer confidence, but this proved to be short lived. Growth did slow again to 2.1% in 2002, due largely to the fall in global economic growth in 2001-2. Most of the 2.1% growth was down to the continued buoyant level of consumer spending. But investment growth collapsed in 2001 and 2003, as did export growth rates. UK imports continued to grow more rapidly than exports due to rising domestic demand. However, mention must also be made of the Labour government, which after keeping a tight rein of the purse strings in the first two years in office, had generated enough of a budget surplus to increase government spending significantly. Between 1999 and 2005, annual real government spending increased by an average rate of 3.2%. This compares to just 0.9% between 1988 and 1997.

2003-7: Steady, stable growth

With geo-political uncertainties receding, the UK picked up again in 2003 and 2004. Business and consumer confidence rebounded and in 2004, investment finally rebounded, reaching a growth rate of 5.7%. Global demand rose significantly in 2003 and 2004, increasing demand for UK exports between 2004 and 2006. The fall in the value of sterling in 2003 also helped the competitiveness of UK exports on world markets. GDP growth in 2004 was 3.0%, rather higher than the gloomy growth figures that had been predicted by many independent economic forecasters. Despite the rise in interest rates from 3.5% in November 2003 to 4.75% by July 2004, consumer spending growth came in at a robust 3.5%, which also helped to suck in imports.

2005 saw a slowing of GDP growth to 2.2%, below the trend rate of growth. Consumer spending growth was much lower, down at 2.3%. The impact of higher interest rates and lower growth of house prices prompted this slowdown in consumer spending. Households began to repay debt accumulated during the previous ten years, indicated by the personal savings ratio edging higher at 5.6%, its second highest value for the period 1999-2007. Investment growth was a disappointing 2.4% that year.

In 2006 and 2007, real GDP grew at 2.9% and 2.6% respectively, very close to trend. Despite a slowdown in government and private sector consumption, investment growth was very impressive (6.5% and 7.8% respectively), while export growth was 11.3% in 2006. It seemed that finally the UK was starting to experience more **balanced growth**. Previously the economy had been far too reliant on consumer spending and, to a lesser extent, a big increase in government spending of 2000-06, to keep GDP growth high. Profligate spending by both consumers and the government meant that both groups accumulated a lot of debt.

2008-9: Recession

Question

2. Explain what is meant by the term i) injection and ii) leakage, using an example of each from the analysis above.

● Analysis: Why did the UK economy go into recession in 2008?

1. The credit crunch.

2. High levels of debt held by UK consumers.

3. The rise in oil prices in 2008.

4. The fall in house prices and share prices in 2008.

1. The credit crunch

A credit crunch is simply when banks stop lending, both to each other and to their customers. Here's how it happened:

(i) Lots of low income US individuals took on large amounts of mortgage debt. They were classed as **sub-prime borrowers** because they were high risk meaning that many were unlikely to be able to pay back the debt. This mortgage debt was repackaged and sold in the debt markets to financial institutions, such as pension funds and hedge funds, all over the world. One person's debt is another person's asset!

(ii) Hedge funds make their money by buying and selling different types of financial assets. Many of their investments were backed up by this repackaged debt.

(iii) It became apparent that a lot of money lent by banks to US sub-prime mortgagors would never get paid back. When financial institutions realised that much of this debt was worthless, banks that had lent money to the hedge funds stopped lending and began to ask for their money back.

(iv) Credit in the markets dried up, and a collapse in confidence occurred in credit markets around the world.

(v) There was then a realisation that risk had been mispriced in many debt markets, including leveraged buyouts – this means buying companies using a significant amount of borrowed money. Banks that lent money for takeovers, such as the takeover of Boots by KKR, were unable to sell on the debt.

(vi) There followed a general collapse in confidence in the financial sector, and banks stopped lending. The decline in bank lending led to a sharp fall in consumer spending and investment in the economy, tipping the economy into recession.

2. High levels of debt held by UK consumers

Many UK consumers and businesses had taken on unsustainable levels of debt in the boom years. This was

partly because central banks, such as the Bank of England and the Federal Reserve in the US, held interest rates too low for too long. Eventually this debt had to be paid off. Households and firms needed to redress their balance sheets, so they began to save more and pay off debt, and spend less.

3. The rise in oil prices in 2008
By July 2008, oil prices had risen to $147, up from $55 a barrel at the beginning of 2007. A significant rise in oil prices shifts the Short Run Aggregate Supply curve to the left, reducing the level of UK GDP.

4. The fall in house prices and share prices in 2008
These two aspects are discussed in Chapters 2 and 4 respectively. But together these two aspects meant that the decline in asset prices reduced household wealth, which resulted in a reduction in consumer spending. This is known as the **wealth effect**.

Question

3. Using aggregate demand and aggregate supply analysis, examine the impact on the UK price level and the level of UK real output of:
   (a) A fall in share prices.
   (b) A rise in the oil price.
   (c) A fall in the level of investment.
   (d) A fall in the rate of growth of house prices.

● Analysis: Economic effects of the 2008-09 recession

- Decline in living standards: incomes for many are falling, leading to a lower standard of living and, in some cases, poverty.

- Rising unemployment: unemployment on the LFS measure (see Chapter 7) has risen from 1.6m in November 2007 to 2.47m by June 2009, and many analysts were predicting that it would peak at 3m. Youth unemployment has risen particularly quickly.

- A decline in job vacancies, leading to a rise in demand for higher education places.

- Declining revenues and profits for businesses, leading to bankruptcies.

- Lower inflation: the CPI (see Chapter 8) declined from 5.2% in September 2008 to 1.6% in August 2009, while the RPI had even become negative.

- A decline in the value of the pound (see Chapter 5).

- A decline in tax revenues for the government, leading to a worsening of the government's finances.

● Analysis: Policies to combat the recession

- Aggressive cuts in interest rates by the Bank of England (see Chapter 9).

- Quantitative easing: increasing the money supply to encourage more lending by banks (see Chapter 9).

- Cuts in taxes, such as the temporary cut in VAT from 17.5% to 15% in December 2008, and an increase in government spending (see Chapter 10).

- Allowing the value of the pound to fall to boost the price competitiveness of UK exports (see Chapter 6).

- More funding for Jobcentre Plus agencies (see Chapter 7).

● Analysis: Economic growth – an international comparison

From the 1960s right up until the mid-1990s, the UK economy experienced a relatively low rate of economic growth compared to its competitors. Reasons cited for this included:

• Low productivity.

• Low investment in fixed capital.

• Low investment in human capital.

• The 'stop-go' or 'boom-bust' nature of the economic cycle.

Figure 1.4: Average annual GDP growth, 1995-2008

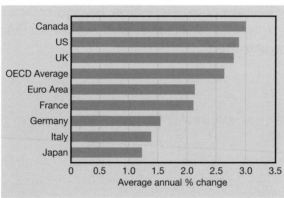

Source: OECD

Although lagging slightly behind the US and Canada, it is notable that since 1995 the UK has outperformed the rest of the G7 nations, as well as the average for the OECD and the Euro Area as shown in Figure 1.4. Both Conservative and Labour governments have introduced supply-side policies to boost investment, innovation and productivity to help account for this impressive growth record which may enable UK growth to continue to increase in the future.

●● Application and Analysis: A breakdown of GDP by categories of expenditure

Figure 1.5: Annual contributions to GDP growth

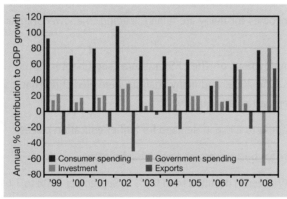

Source: Calculated from ONS data

Figure 1.5 and Table 1.1 show the contributions to GDP growth of consumer spending, investment, government spending and net exports. The tall blue bars clearly show that the UK economy was heavily reliant on consumer spending in order to maintain growth. Government spending was more important in this time period than in the 1990s, while the contribution of net exports has been *negative*. In fact, in 2005 and 2006, exports alone contributed more to growth than the chart indicates. This is because the chart depicts **net exports** (value of exports

– value of imports) and imports have been rising faster than exports! As a contributor to growth investment has been largely subdued and only contributed sporadically to growth. We noted earlier in 1998, strong growth and again between 2004 and 2006 when it was actually making the largest contribution to growth. It is also notable that in 2008, investment growth collapsed as businesses first forecast, and then experienced, declining demand for their products. It seems then that for this period, UK growth was very unbalanced, driven largely by rising consumer spending and borrowing.

Table 1.1: Average shares of GDP by main category* 1997-2008, real terms

Component of GDP	Share of GDP
Household Final Consumer Spending	61.3%
Investment	16.7%
Government Spending	21.2%
Net Exports	-2.2%

Source: ONS. *Note: These figures do not total to 100 as spending by non-profit institutions and changes in inventories have been omitted.

Example of evaluation technique

Evaluate the importance of a macroeconomic variable by looking at its share of GDP

Consumer spending has always been the most important aspect of GDP and is typically 60% or over for most industrialised economies. Therefore it is not surprising that a lot of attention is paid to consumer behaviour. However, it is the extent to which consumer spending is driving growth that remains the concern. Further, Figure 1.5 indicates that the next most important aspect of GDP is government spending. GDP growth has been driven by both private and, to a lesser extent, public sector spending, which have in turn been fuelled by debt. Investment spending and net exports have had consistently low shares of total spending. It is essential for long term growth prospects that investment and exports take up the slack as the government and private sector households seek to redress their balance sheets.

Application and Analysis: Sectors of the economy

Figure 1.6: The UK – a three speed economy?

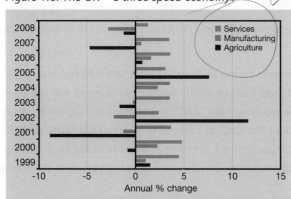

Source: ONS

The aggregate GDP growth figures mask the very different speeds at which the different sectors of the UK economy have been growing.

Figure 1.6 suggests that the UK could be described as a three speed economy. The service sector has been growing continually over the last ten years while manufacturing growth has been consistently lower. Agriculture, in contrast, has been in recession several times over the last ten years.

The reasons for the sluggish growth in manufacturing output between 1998 and 2003 include:

- The sustained rise in the value of the pound against the dollar and the euro between 1996 and 2000, making UK manufactured exports less price competitive. This is especially significant as a large proportion of manufactured output is exported abroad. However, the worst period for manufacturing came later in 2001-2, when the value of the pound then began to fall.

- The global economic downturn in 2001-2: In 2001 economic growth in the UK's two most important export markets, the US and Germany, was only 0.8% and 1.4% respectively.

The service sector, by contrast, is less dependent on international trade and more dependent upon the state of the domestic economy. For the last ten years, UK growth has been driven by the service sector: much of the growth in real output can be accounted for by growth in output in financial services and distribution, hotel and catering. Between 1998 and 2008, rising consumer spending and relatively low unemployment led to growth in the service sector of 3.6% on average. The pace of service sector expansion slowed slightly in 2002-3, however. This was partly due to sluggish growth in the transport industry, especially air transport, and in other industries dependent on overseas travel and tourism. The financial intermediation sector was also growing very slowly in 2002 and 2003, reflecting financial market volatility and general economic uncertainty at the time. But since 2003, financial services have experienced the most rapid rise in output of all services, followed by transport and communication and distribution. Construction output growth had been impressive but grew less rapidly in 2005 and 2006. The worst year for agriculture was of course 2001, precipitated by the foot and mouth crisis that started in February that year. The severity of the 2008-9 recession was such that all sectors began to experience declining output

after the third quarter of 2008. Manufacturing, construction and financial services experienced a particularly severe decline.

● Evaluation: A 'V' shaped or 'W' shaped recession?

In a speech in October 2004 the governor of the Bank of England, Mervyn King, described the period 1995-2004 as the *nice* decade (non inflationary consistent expansion).[2] The 2008-9 recession has been anything but nice for the homeowners, workers and businesses who have suffered. At the time of writing (late in 2009), the preliminary third quarter GDP figures for 2009 were again negative, indicating that the 2008-9 recession was the longest and deepest since 1955. However, there was also some tentative cause for optimism:

- Surveys were indicating greater business confidence.

- Businesses were starting to run down their stocks and would soon have to kick-start production to satisfy demand.

- The decline in UK output had begun to slow down. Many forecasters were predicting that the fourth quarter of 2009 could see growth.

This optimistic view is that the economy will come out of recession and then grow continually: there would be a 'V' shaped recession.

However, other commentators were saying that once businesses had run out of stocks, the fact that consumers still have to rebuild their balance sheets means that demand will not be forthcoming. Spare capacity will lead to a collapse in investment, and the economy will go back into recession. Further, inflationary pressures might induce the Bank of England to raise interest rates, while the government will soon have to raise taxes and cut government spending in order to repay its mounting debts. This would then result in a W or 'double dip' recession. Only time will tell which group of commentators was right.

Harder Questions

4. Explain why the UK economy has a business cycle, as shown in Figure 1.2 (hint: use the concepts of the accelerator, the multiplier and inventories in your answer).

5. To what extent has UK economic growth between 1997 and 2007 been unbalanced?

---

2. Speech at the Eden Project, Cornwall, 12 October 2004, full text available from www.bankofengland.co.uk.

Chapter 2
Consumer Spending and Saving

In this Chapter we consider in detail the movement of household expenditure during the past decade and the factors which seem to explain the different rates of growth in spending. These include interest rate changes and the personal sector wealth effects.

● Knowledge: Economic theory and consumption

Several economists have developed theories relating to the level of consumption expenditure.

• John Maynard Keynes
Keynes argued in his **absolute income hypothesis** that the most important determinant of current consumption is current real disposable income. As disposable income increases, consumer spending increases, but by less than the increase in disposable income. Although the variables are closely correlated, as we shall see, for certain time periods the actual observations are significantly different from that predicted by Keynes' consumption function. Also, consumer spending tends to fluctuate less over the business cycle than disposable income. More sophisticated models are therefore needed to explain fully changes in consumer spending.

• Franco Modigliani
Modigliani's **life cycle hypothesis** suggests that people attempt to smooth out consumer spending over their lifetime. When people are young, they borrow heavily to finance the purchase of a house and the raising of a family, for example. They do this because they know they will be able to earn more in the future. They borrow now, knowing they can pay back later. In middle age, when they are earning more, they pay off the debts they ran up when they were young and save in order to prepare for retirement. During retirement, people spend more than they earn and run down their savings.

• Milton Friedman
Friedman's **permanent income hypothesis** suggests that the key determinant of consumer spending is an individual's permanent income. Permanent income is the value of everything a person owns, including physical wealth (a house, company shares, government bonds) and human wealth (the value of an individual's education and skills). It approximates to the average income of an individual over his/her lifetime. Friedman suggested that consumers try to smooth out consumer spending based on their estimates of their permanent income. Only if there is a change in permanent income will there be a change in consumer spending. Any change in income perceived as transitory or temporary, such as a cut in taxes just prior to an election, will not change consumer spending.

Both Modigliani and Friedman's theories suggest that a temporary or unexpected increase in income is either saved, or that the extra consumer spending is spread over the rest of the life cycle.

• James Duesenberry
Duesenberry's **relative income hypothesis** argues that people's spending today is determined by the living standards of others and their own past experience. Poor individuals save at a lower rate than rich ones because society as a whole sets standards of spending that everyone, including the poor, feels they have to meet. Consumer spending falls less than income during recessions because people find it hard to cut spending back from the levels they were previously used to.

Question

1. Which two of the following are most likely to lead to a rise in an individual's permanent income?
   (a) A fall in house prices.
   (b) A fall in interest rates.
   (c) A rise in share prices.
   (d) A fall in income tax rates.
   (e) The individual achieving a First Class Honours Degree in Economics.

● ● Application and Analysis: Explaining changes in consumer spending

Figure 2.1: Growth of households' real consumer expenditure

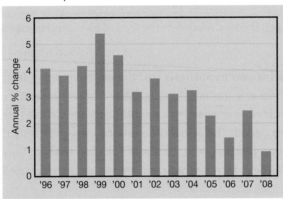

Source: ONS

Figure 2.2: UK consumer spending and disposable income

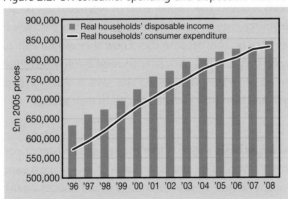

Source: ONS

Figure 2.3: Growth of UK real consumer spending and real disposable income

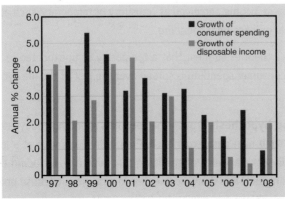

Source: ONS

As noted in Chapter 1 consumer spending is the most important component of GDP in the UK economy. It accounted for 62% of total UK GDP in real terms in 2008. Changes in consumer spending have a significant impact on GDP growth: indeed the UK economy largely has the consumer to thank for its impressive GDP growth over the period 1997-2007.

Figure 2.1 reveals strong growth of consumer spending between 1996 and 2004. We can identify four reasons for this outcome. They are rising real disposable incomes, low interest rates, rising personal sector wealth and falling real prices of consumer durable goods. We consider each of these in turn.

1. Rising real disposable incomes

During this period there was a sustained rise in real disposable income, which grew by 4.2% in both 1996 and 2000, and 4.5% in 2001. Cuts in the basic rate and starting rate of income tax boosted disposable income, while earned income also grew over the period. There is indeed some evidence for the absolute income hypothesis. In Figure 2.2 real disposable income and real consumer spending closely track one another, while Figure 2.3 indicates strong consumer spending growth when disposable income growth is high, such as in 1997, 2000 and 2001, and vice versa, such as in 2005 and 2006.

● Evaluation: The current income-spending relationship

However, in 1998-9, 2002, 2004 and 2007, when disposable income growth was more modest, consumer spending growth was well in excess of that of disposable income. This could provide some evidence for the relative income hypothesis. In contrast, in 2008 consumer spending growth is barely half that of disposable income. There is clearly more than just current income that is determining UK consumer spending. In particular, notice how in Figure 2.2 the purple line closes in on the top of the orange bars!

2. Low interest rates

Figure 2.4: The savings ratio of UK households

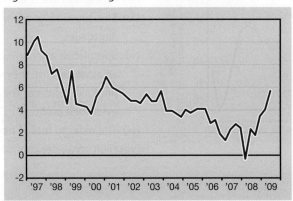

Source: ONS

Figure 2.5: Consumer spending on durables and bank rate

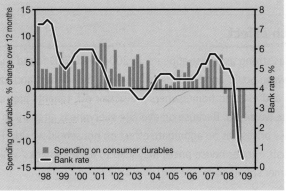

Source: ONS

The Bank of England base rate was very low between 1998 and 2004 in comparison to the 1980s and early 1990s. The fall in interest rates, which began in 1998, helped consumer spending growth to surge beyond the growth in disposable income. After the third quarter of 1997, the savings ratio (Figure 2.4) began to fall. It is clear that low interest rates helped to increase consumer confidence and induced many individuals to borrow more to finance consumer spending.

There is some evidence of a *lagged relationship* between interest rates and spending on consumer durables, as shown in Figure 2.5. Changes in interest rates take time to have an effect on aggregate demand in the economy through the **transmission mechanism** (see Chapter 9). Successive interest rate rises in 1997 led to consumers cutting back spending on durables in 1998. Lower interest rates in 1998-9 lead to a rebound in spending in 1999-2001, while hikes in interest rates from the end of 1999 into 2000 lead to a slowdown in spending in 2002.

● Evaluation: Interest rates too low?

Most economists agree that low interest rates were a particularly significant cause of high consumer spending during 1997-2007. By historical standards interest rates were indeed very low. There is a consensus that the main reason for the boom-bust cycle was that central banks around the world, including the Bank of England, kept interest rates too low for too long.

3. Rising personal sector wealth

Figure 2.6 indicates some impressive house price growth, especially in 2000 and 2002-3. The rise in house prices contributed to a rise in the value of personal sector wealth, which increases consumer spending via the **wealth effect**. There are several ways in which this can be explained:

- Individuals may have spent more simply because they 'felt' wealthier.
- A rise in house prices increases an individual's permanent income, which should increase consumer spending.
- The period 1997-2007 also saw a significant rise in **mortgage equity withdrawal**: people borrowing more money secured against the rising value of their properties. Figure 2.6 highlights the extent of this recent increase. This also helped to boost consumer spending.

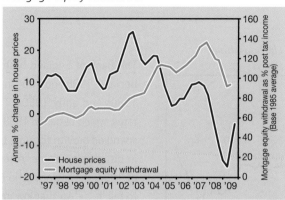

Figure 2.6: Growth of UK house prices and mortgage equity withdrawal

Source: Nationwide

Why did house prices rise so rapidly between 1997 and 2007?

(i)   Strong real income growth.

(ii) Low interest rates.

(iii) Falling and low unemployment.

(iv) The growing availability of fixed rate mortgages.

(v)   Speculative activity – people purchasing an asset because they expect it to rise in price in the future. They can then sell the asset for a profit.

(vi) The reduced fear of **negative equity**.

(vii) High consumer confidence.

Question

2. Using your knowledge of Economics, explain how each of the factors above would lead to a rise in UK house prices.

● Evaluation of the wealth effect

The wealth effect may not be as strong as it first appears. In 2004 the OECD found that if wealth rises by $1, spending only rises between $0.01 and $0.07. Further, there are winners and losers from higher house prices. Whilst landlords and existing homeowners are better off, tenants are no better off and prospective first time buyers are worse off. Because on average everyone is a tenant in their own home until they die, a change in house prices has no aggregate effect on household wealth. However, houses can be used as security on a loan. Higher house prices may lead to a rise in banks' willingness to lend, which may well increase consumer spending.[1]

4. Falling real prices of consumer durables

A further determinant of spending on durables is, of course, the price of the goods themselves! This has been falling in recent years due to the emergence of low cost producers such as China and India, from whom the UK has been importing durables more cheaply than they could be made within the UK.

The period 2003-7 saw a slight slowdown in the rate of growth of consumer spending. Given low interest rates, high house prices and relatively low unemployment the dominant explanation for slower consumer spending would appear to be the slowdown in the rate of growth of disposable income. Slower economic growth generally as well as increases in employee National Insurance Contributions and Council Tax in 2002-3 may have played their part. The decline in consumer spending growth in 2005-8 seems to be explained by rising interest rates: in particular, four quarter point rises between November 2003 and July 2004, and five quarter point rises from July 2006 to July 2007. House price growth did decline in 2005-6, so there may have been a negative wealth effect, although equity withdrawal was still robust.

---

1. 'Economics Focus: Home Truths', *The Economist*, 7 August 2008.

● Evaluation: How important is unemployment as a determinant of consumer spending?

The period 1996-2000 witnessed a very rapid decline in the unemployment rate. Rapid economic growth boosted the demand for labour and as a result the claimant count rate virtually halved from 7% to 3%. Precautionary saving became less as more individuals were working and earning higher wages, and individuals spent more. 2004 and 2005 saw a slight rise in unemployment, but thereafter it remained stable until 2008. However, consumer spending growth was much more volatile than this, suggesting that unemployment is perhaps a less important determinant of consumer spending at the macro level than the others. However, the *threat of unemployment* has often been argued in the past as an important determinant of household saving.

Figure 2.7: Nationwide consumer confidence index

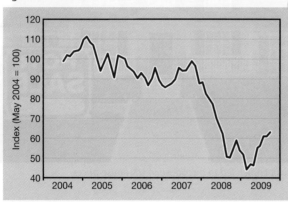

Source: Nationwide

Consumer confidence is an important *leading* or *predictive indicator* of consumer spending in the economy. Figure 2.7 shows that this has generally been on a downward trend since 2004, although there was an upward blip in 2007. This index is calculated from a sample survey, in which consumers are asked their feelings about the current economic situation and the current employment situation, both now and in 6 months time, and expectations about household income in 6 months time.

● Analysis: Why did consumer spending growth collapse in 2008-09?

Figure 2.8 illustrates the sharp decline in consumer spending growth in the economy, from a robust 2.8% growth rate in the third quarter of 2007 to a negative one of -3.6% by the second quarter of 2009. The reasons for this include:

• The fall in real disposable income. Economic recession has squeezed household incomes, largely because businesses have enforced pay cuts or freezes, and City bonuses have been reduced. This has forced consumers to cut back expenditure.

Figure 2.8: Annual change in real household consumer expenditure

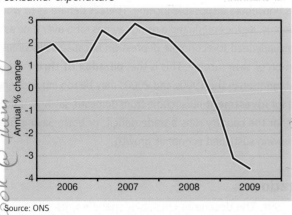

Source: ONS

• House prices grew too high. The ratio of house prices to average earnings rose from a low of 3.5 in the mid 1990s to 6.5 by the beginning of 2007. The ratio of house prices to rental income also grew rapidly. People were prepared to pay high prices because they were buying houses for speculative reasons, i.e. so they could sell the house for a profit, rather than purchasing based on what the houses were really worth. This was the classic sign of a **bubble**, and house prices ended up over-valued. The hikes in interest rates from 4.5% in July 2006 to 5.75% in June 2007, the realisation that prices were overvalued, and the credit crunch led to a collapse in UK house prices. This led to a negative wealth effect.

• Negative equity and debt overhang. In 2008-9 many households faced the situation of negative equity:

Overvalued houses added to the credit crunch led to a collapse in UK house prices.

where the value of their house was worth less than the value of their mortgage debt. Households now have to repay the money they borrowed in the boom years.

• Higher unemployment, and the threat of unemployment, have combined to reduce spending and increase precautionary saving.

• The impact of the credit crunch made borrowing more difficult: banks became less willing to lend.

• The rise in the price of oil and food in 2008 increased the cost of necessities and forced consumers to cut back significantly on consumer durables (as shown in Figure 2.5).

● Knowledge: Saving

Saving is any part of household disposable income that is not consumed. The **savings ratio** is household savings as a percentage of gross household disposable income. There is debate as to whether a high or low savings ratio is good for the economy. Keynes predicted a rising savings ratio over time as income increased. He argued that this would eventually lead to economic depression because as incomes grew, individuals spent a lower and lower proportion of their income. This is the '**paradox of thrift**' argument. One of the reasons for Japan's prolonged stagnation in the 1990s and 2000s may be too much saving and not enough spending. However, the finance for **investment** must come from domestic savings, unless the government runs a persistent budget deficit, or the country runs a trade deficit, or both. Saving finances investment, and investment is crucial in achieving sustained economic growth.

● Application: The savings ratio

A lack of savings and underinvestment has often been highlighted as a fundamental structural weakness of the UK economy. Between 1997 and 2008, the UK savings ratio declined on trend, as Figure 2.4 demonstrates. The UK household savings ratio is also below the OECD average (Figure 2.9). However, countries with higher savings ratios, such as Germany and Italy, have more rapidly ageing populations than the UK, so our requirement to save may be considerably less.

Figure 2.9: International comparison of household savings ratio, %

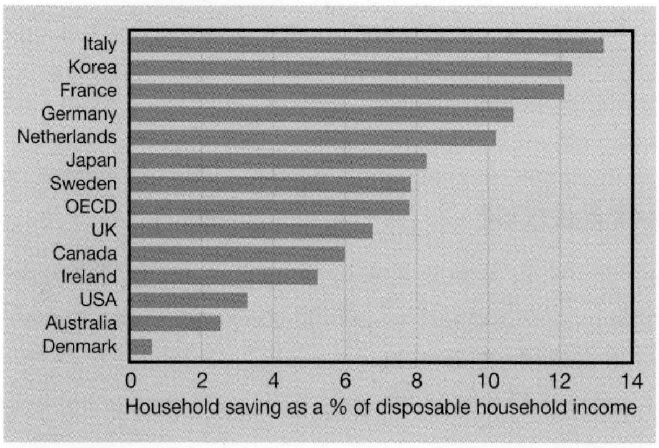

Household saving as a % of disposable household income

Source: OECD

● Analysis: Why did the savings ratio decline between 1997 and 2008?

Three factors explain the falling savings ratio.

- Interest rates were low by historical standards, reducing the incentive to save and increasing the incentive to borrow and spend. Growth of incomes coupled with low interest rates increased the affordability of housing. Many people took on large amounts of mortgage debt to get on the 'housing ladder'.

- The growth of house prices increased the incentive to spend rather than save.

- Unemployment was relatively low and stable, reducing the amount of precautionary saving. Consumer confidence was also high during the period.

● Analysis: Why did the savings ratio increase in 2009?

Here again several factors explain the reversal in the movement of the savings ratio.

- Debt hangover: consumers are finally starting to repay the debt accumulated during the boom years.

- Lower house prices have caused a **negative wealth effect**, reducing consumer spending and increasing saving.

- Higher unemployment, and the **threat of unemployment**, has increased precautionary saving.

The government is concerned at the lack of saving in the UK, and has introduced some initiatives to save, especially for retirement. These include:

- The introduction of the stakeholder pension scheme for low income workers. However, the take up has been slow.

- The introduction of the pension credit in 2003. This is a means-tested scheme to top up benefits for poor pensioners.

- The replacement of TESSAs (Tax Exempt Special Savings Accounts) and PEPs (personal Equity Plans) with ISAs (Individual Savings Accounts) in 1999.

- The income individuals earn from the interest on the savings or the equity plan is tax free. From April 2010, the total yearly amount individuals can invest will be £10,200 per year, of which £5,100 can be in cash. Over 18 million people have invested in ISAs since 1999.

Question

3. To what extent should the fact that the UK savings ratio is below the OECD average be a cause for concern?

Question – Spreadsheet Exercise

1. Go to the Office for National Statistics website at www.statistics.gov.uk. Download the annual data for real household disposable income and real household consumer expenditure for the UK for the years 1970-2008 and place in columns A, B and C of your spreadsheet. (Place the years in Column A, making sure each year is preceded by an apostrophe ['].) Graph the data of household spending and disposable income in a scatter plot.

   HINT: highlight the data. Then go to Insert, Scatter, and select the first option.

   Give your graph a title, and label the axes. HINT: click on the chart, then go to Layout in Chart Tools. THEN click on Axes title and Chart title.

2. Find the equation of the line of best fit, i.e. the consumption function.

   HINT: right click anywhere on your observations (the blue dots!) on your graph and select 'Add trendline' and assume the relationship between the two variables is linear.

   Tick the boxes that say 'Display equation on chart' and 'Display R squared option on chart'.

3. The R squared gives us the percentage of variations in consumption that can be explained by the variations in income. What is the value of the R squared for this data?

4. What is the value of the Average Propensity to Consume a) in 1970, b) in 2006?

   HINT: (Calculate Total Consumer Expenditure/Total Disposable Income and put in column D.)

5. At first glance, the model looks to fit the Keynesian theory rather well. However, what if we plot the **error terms**?

   In column E, use a formula to calculate the predicted value of consumer expenditure from the consumption function equation for each year.

   HINT: for 1970, put the actual value of disposable income into the equation you worked out in 2. That is the value of x, you can then calculate the value of y. You need to insert a formula in cell E2 that you can copy and paste down to E40.

6. Calculate the error terms, Column C *minus* Column E, and put in column F. The error terms show us the deviation of actual consumption from that forecast by the line of best fit.

7. Graph the **error terms** (Column F) on a column graph against time (Column A).

   HINT: highlight A2-A38 and F2-F38 (use ctrl button to highlight two columns together), go to Insert Column and again select the first graph option. Cut and paste graph into Word document.

8. Explain how you **might** account for the large **negative** errors between 1991 and 1997, and the large **positive** errors between 2002 and 2006?

   HINT: what might have been happening to other determinants of consumer spending at that time?

9. **Evaluate** whether current income is the main determinant of current consumption.

Chapter 3

UK Business and Industry

In this Chapter we consider the fall in the relative importance of the manufacturing sector in the UK – the process of deindustrialisation and the reasons that account for it. The Chapter includes coverage of government policies to assist manufacturing industry, corporate profitability, business investment and inward flows of foreign direct investment.

● ● Knowledge and Application: The decline of manufacturing

Manufacturing today only accounts for 12.4% of UK output. The service sector, in contrast, now accounts for 76% of UK output and over 80% of UK employment. The UK is thus now a 'post industrial' or information economy.

In the last thirty years, the UK has suffered a decline in the share of output and employment accounted for by the manufacturing sector (Table 3.1). This phenomenon is known as **deindustrialisation**. However, labour productivity in UK manufacturing has improved considerably (see Chapter 6). This has been due to higher investment in fixed capital equipment, IT and the skills of the workforce. Nonetheless, the UK has surrendered its comparative advantage in many manufacturing sectors, though it retains a comparative advantage in pharmaceuticals.

Table 3.1: Deindustrialisation in the UK

	Manufacturing Output, % Total	Manufacturing Workforce Jobs, % Total	Service Sector Output, % Total	Service Sector Workforce Jobs, % total
1979	28.0	26.0	60%	62.0
1990	22.5	17.8	64.1	70.4
2007	12.4	10.1	76.1	80.7

Source: ONS

Figure 3.1 illustrates the contrasting growth performance of mining, quarrying and manufacturing compared to the other sectors. In fact, manufacturing output declined in 2001-3, 2005 and 2008-2009Q2. Two reasons cited for the recession in manufacturing in 2001-3 were:
• The slowdown in global economic growth.
• The strength of the pound sterling that hampered export competitiveness.

Both the machine tools industry and the clothing and textiles sector were hit particularly hard because of the strength of the pound in the late 1990s. Other industries hit during the 2001-3 recession include:
• Aerospace manufacturing;
• Computer manufacturing;
• Office equipment;
• Electrical engineering; and
• Telecommunications engineering.

In 2005, transport equipment and electrical goods were two other industries to suffer. In 2006, however, manufacturing growth rebounded. UK manufacturing is heavily dependant upon exports, and a growing

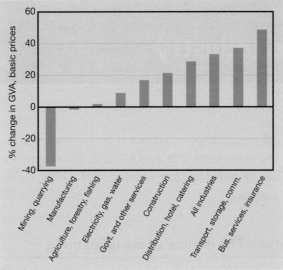

Figure 3.1: Growth of UK industries by sector, 1999-2008

Source: ONS. GVA is Gross Value Added: for our purposes the same as GDP

world economy in 2006, as well as an unexpected fall in the oil price in the second half of the year, helped in the recovery.

However, manufacturing, like all other sectors, has experienced a collapse in output during the 2008-9 recession, although it has been hit harder than most service sector industries in terms of loss of output and job losses. Anecdotal evidence suggests that car manufacturing, as well as industries that supply the car industry, engineering and textiles have suffered particularly. The construction industry also experienced a particularly sharp fall in output in 2008-9, having shown strong growth over the previous ten years as is evident from Figure 3.1.

● Analysis: Why has deindustrialisation occurred?

- In a 'mature' economy such as the UK, consumer demand inevitably switches away from manufactures towards services: services have a higher **income elasticity of demand** than manufactures.

- Foreign competition from regions such as East Asia and Latin America means that the UK no longer has a **comparative advantage** in manufactures. As much of UK manufactured output is traded then manufactured output growth will be slow.

Figure 3.2: Index of output of selected industries, 2005 = 100

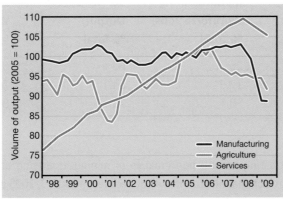

Source: OECD

Given that a similar process has occurred in other developed market economies, the slow rate of growth of the manufacturing sector does not initially seem a cause for concern. It should also be noted from Figure 3.2 that it was not until the 2008-9 recession that the UK manufacturing sector was really contracting. What Figure 3.2 shows clearly is that it is the **share** of output accounted for by manufacturing that has been falling over the long term. Note the continuous rise in the output of the service sector over the ten year period 1998-2008.

● Evaluation: Does manufacturing matter?

Nonetheless, some commentators have claimed that manufacturing is more important that its 12.4% of GDP suggests and deserves special treatment. The reasons are as follows:

- There is greater scope for productivity improvements, innovation and technological improvements in manufacturing than in the service sector. This is because the service sector is labour intensive and there is little scope for capital-labour substitution, making technological change difficult to implement.

 - Most research and development (R&D) in the private sector is conducted in manufacturing: it is responsible for around 75% of UK R&D.[1] R&D is becoming a more significant determinant of growth in

1. Figures from www.dti.gov.uk/manufacturing.

the industrialised economies. A healthy manufacturing sector will mean innovation, productivity improvements and therefore increased long term economic growth. Given that the UK still has a productivity gap with its major competitors, this argument seems difficult to ignore.

- Manufacturing accounts for 60% of UK exports of goods and services. One of the reasons for the UK's chronic or structural current account deficit is the decline in the value of manufactured exports relative to imports. However, the deficit in goods can be made up by other factors such as investment income and services. This is true up to a point: however, the UK is also likely to remain a net importer of primary products as well as manufactures. Taken together, the deficit in these areas has tended to outweigh the surplus in services and investment income.

- Manufacturing generates millions of jobs both directly and indirectly through the supply chain. In fact, manufacturing has more forward and backward linkages than any other sector of the economy.

On the other hand, the assertion that the UK economy simply doesn't make anything any more does not stand up to scrutiny. In absolute terms, the volume of UK manufacturing output in 2007 was at a record high, twice the 1955 figure. The UK has lost its comparative advantage in traditional manufactures such as textiles and shipbuilding, but has since 'traded up' to higher value added manufactures. The UK remains a world leader in certain hi-tech industries: for example, eight out of the twelve Formula 1 teams scheduled to be on the grid for the start of the 2010 season base their teams in the UK! There is also nothing wrong with the UK importing tangible goods in exchange for exporting non tangibles, such as financial services exports. It should be noted, however, that our trade deficit in goods is larger than our trade surplus in services (see Chapter 5).

Questions

1. What is meant by the phrase 'index of output… 2005 = 100'?

2. With reference to Figure 3.2, describe the changes in output of agriculture, manufacturing and services between 1998 and 2009.

Extension material: Government policy to assist manufacturing

Given the importance of manufacturing in the UK, and its decline, in 2002 the Department for Trade and Industry (DTI) published a Manufacturing Strategy, which set out a framework for UK manufacturers, government and trade unions to enhance the competitiveness of UK manufacturing. The plan identified seven 'pillars' necessary for success:

(i) Macroeconomic stability.

(ii) Investment.

(iii) Science and innovation.

(iv) Best practice (raising productivity and competitiveness by continuous improvement).

(v) Skills and education.

(vi) Modern infrastructure.

(vii) The right market framework (providing the business environment manufacturing needs to compete globally).

Two years later, in July 2004, the DTI reported back on how these priorities have been implemented. Policies have included:

- The launch of the Manufacturing Advisory Service (MAS). This helps manufacturers, large and small, identify sources of manufacturing related support. There is an MAS for each region and they operate in association with regional business links, universities and so on.
- Skills and training improvements, including Modern Apprenticeships and Sector skills councils.
- Promoting R&D via the introduction of the R&D tax credit.

- Heavy government investment in science and research.
- Setting up innovation and growth teams in key manufacturing sectors.

The government hopes that the MAS will enable more companies to move to a world class standard by constantly innovating and investing in new products, new designs, new materials and new production techniques. However manufacturing output growth in the 2000s has been slow and, as we have seen, the sector has frequently been in recession. As firms have failed to pass on rising costs in the form of rising prices, margins have been squeezed and manufacturers are looking to cut back investment, especially in 2008-9.

To help the ailing car industry, the government in 2009 announced loans of up to £1.3bn from the European Investment Bank and a further £1bn in UK government loans. £100m funding was made available for the training of car manufacturing workers. The government also introduced a car scrappage scheme which allows anyone who trades in a car that is more than 10 years old a £2,000 payment if they buy a new one.

However, it could be argued that the first three measures do not get to the heart of the problem, which is lack of demand for cars. But the scrappage scheme has stimulated demand for new cars and helped reduce carbon emissions, since new cars are 'greener' than old ones.

● ● Knowledge and Application: The service sector

Between 1997 and 2001, the fastest growing sector of the UK economy was transport and communications. However, the growth rate in this sector has subsided since then. In 2003-7, the business service sector showed more consistently high growth than transport and communications, and continued to grow strongly, though growth in this sector also fell in 2001-2. Following the decision to raise government spending substantially in 2000-6, government services grew rapidly and consistently over this period. Distribution, hotel and catering growth was also strong throughout the period. However, all of these industries mentioned above suffered a slowdown during 2001-2.

Figure 3.3: Change in output Q1 2008 - Q2 2009, various sectors

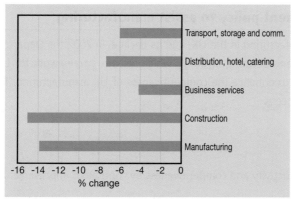

Source: ONS

During the recession of 2008-9, all service sectors suffered a fall in output. The fall was sharp, except in the case of government services. Financial services and transport, storage and communication experienced particularly sharp falls in output, although nowhere near as sharp as manufacturing and construction (Figure 3.3). The volume of retail sales has also held up fairly well in 2008-9.

The banking sector suffered particularly in the 2008-9 recession, particularly banks that relied heavily on the mortgage market. These banks still have a lot of bad debts which are debts that are very unlikely to ever be paid back. Northern Rock was nationalised in February 2008, while the government also took a 43% stake in Lloyds Banking Group in January 2009 and a 70% stake in Bradford and Bingley in April 2009. In addition, in 2008 the Bank of England had a £50bn plan to allow commercial banks to swap risky mortgage debt for secure government debt. Late in 2009 some banks less reliant on mortgages such as HSBC and Barclays began to report a recovery in profits, but Northern Rock and Lloyds were still struggling.

Question

3. Evaluate the assertion that the decisions to prop up the UK car and banking industries were justified.

Knowledge: Corporate profitability

Company profitability is essential in determining the health of the UK corporate sector, and the performance of the economy as a whole.

- Around 70% of UK capital investment spending is financed out of retained profit; that is, profit after taxes and dividends.

- Firms invest in order to expand and make profit: thus profit acts as a source of finance and a reward for investment.

- Higher profits may be paid out to shareholders in the form of dividends, which may increase consumer spending in the future, and will lead to higher tax receipts for the central government, improving the public finances.

- Higher profits may reflect lower costs, greater efficiency and greater productivity.

Application and Analysis: UK profitability during the decade

Figure 3.4: Corporate profitability in the UK – return on capital employed

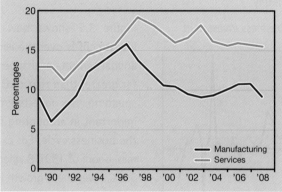

Source: ONS.   Net profit/capital employed.

Figure 3.4 indicates a cyclical pattern of net profitability. The period 1993-97 saw a rise in the profitability of manufacturing and services. This was due to the recovery of the UK economy in this period, which was initially export-led (1993-5) and then consumer-led (1996-7). The lower sterling foreign exchange rate meant that companies were able to keep foreign prices constant and take a bigger margin in sterling terms. Devaluation reduces the price of exports in foreign currency terms. However, exporters may choose to increase the sterling price rather than reduce the foreign currency price. Volumes remain unchanged, so export values rise. This is what happened in the UK from 1993-5.

Service sector profitability was also buoyant during this period. However, as the chart shows, profitability fell slightly in 1998 and 1999. Manufacturing profitability fell largely due to the increase in the value of the pound, while price wars in many service sector industries kept service sector profitability from rising.

During 2000-2, profitability continued to fall further. Reasons cited included low labour productivity growth, the continued strength of the pound compared to the euro and low levels of investment.

In fact all of these reasons were rejected by two government economists who claimed their research indicated that there is no historic statistical link between either productivity, or the exchange rate, and profitability.[2] It is also likely that weak profits in 2001 reduced investment rather than the other way round.

Between 2003-7, profitability rebounded again, as the UK economy continued to experience stable economic growth. The profitability survey cited above found that the UK corporate sector was in a healthy situation in an international context. In a survey of 34 developed market economies, the UK ranks fifth highest on service sector profitability and fourth highest for overall profitability. But the UK was only 13th in the profitability of manufacturing, indicating that the DTI's Manufacturing Strategy, introduced in the same year, has much to do. Indeed, UK companies cannot afford to be complacent. In today's ever more competitive and globalised marketplace, companies cannot rely on annual price hikes in order to maintain

2. L. Citron and R. Walton, 'International Comparisons of Profitability', *Economic Trends*, Vol. 587, October 2002.

profitability. Rather, they will have to cut costs and boost efficiency and productivity in order to compete. UK businesses have often been criticised for too much **short-termism**, and a lack of fixed capital investment, which of course is one way to boost productivity and profitability.

● Knowledge: Investment

Fixed Capital Investment is defined by economists as spending on capital goods, plant, machinery and tools in order to increase the productive capacity of either the individual firm or the economy as a whole.

Fixed capital investment means that firms are able to:
- Increase capacity.
- Gain economies of scale.
- Increase efficiency and boost labour productivity.
- Increase profitability and competitiveness.

Investment is also crucial to the performance of the macroeconomy. It is an **injection into the circular flow of income** and a component of aggregate demand; thus, a rise in investment will boost domestic demand and national income, in the short term, via the **multiplier effect**. Investment also increases the capacity of the economy to supply more goods and services over the long term, therefore increasing long run aggregate supply in the economy.

Figure 3.5: The volatility of UK business investment

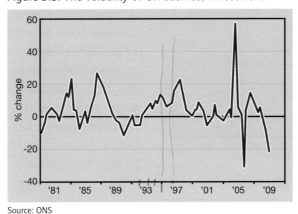

Source: ONS

Figure 3.5 shows how volatile business investment is over the economic cycle. The annual percentage changes in investment are far greater than that of GDP and consumer spending, so investment may be more important in accounting for fluctuations in the business cycle. For example, during the mini boom of 1997-8 when GDP growth was 3.6%, investment growth increased from 5% to 22%! During the slowdown of 2001-2, when GDP growth fell back to 2% (although GDP *levels* didn't fall), business investment growth became negative, i.e. investment levels fell.

● Analysis: Why did the UK have an investment boom in 1997-8?

(i)   The **accelerator** theory of investment suggests that the level of investment is determined by past changes in aggregate demand. The mini boom in 1997-8 led to a rise in investment, as firms that were reaching capacity constraints expanded capacity to benefit from growing demand for goods and services. Investment is highly *pro-cyclical*, and it is also a *lagged indicator*.

(ii) By the late 1990s, however, expectations of high inflation, which had persisted in the 1980s and early 1990s had receded as the economy began to experience years of low and stable inflation. In 1998, the UK economy experienced a mini investment boom, although not on the scale of that of the US.

(iii) High and rising levels of corporate profitability.

(iv) Low interest rates in the late 1990s than previous years meant that debt finance was cheaper.

Between 1999 and 2002, slightly weaker demand and lower corporate profitability, combined with greater levels of uncertainty following the global slowdown and the 11 September 2001 terrorist attacks in New York meant that business investment levels fell, i.e. investment growth became negative.

From 2004-6, investment growth increased, and by the end of 2007 UK investment had reached its most impressive growth rate since 1998. The gentle closing of the output gap meant that some firms reached capacity constraints. Higher GDP growth and corporate profitability boosted business confidence, though manufacturing profitability remained weak as shown in Figure 3.4. The upturn in investment helped sustain UK GDP as well as helping UK GDP growth to become more *balanced*. But with the arrival of recession in 2008, businesses have cut back investment due to lower aggregate demand and the drying up of bank lending.

● Knowledge: Foreign Direct Investment

Foreign Direct Investment (FDI) is where a multinational company takes a 'lasting interest' in a company located in a foreign country.[3] This could include a foreign company setting up a plant in the UK, or engaging in a joint venture with either a domestic private sector company or the government. Often it involves a cross border merger or acquisition of a domestic company by a foreign multinational. FDI is extremely important to the UK economy and the total stock of inward FDI now accounts for a quarter of UK GDP.

● Analysis: The benefits of FDI for the UK economy

- As with domestic investment, FDI represents an injection into the circular flow of income, and causes a multiplied increase in national income.

- It provides jobs, both directly and indirectly through the supply chain. In 2000, multinationals employed almost two million people in the UK economy.

- FDI can lead to an improvement in the balance of payments. The initial FDI is a **credit** on the **financial account**, and if the multinational exports its products abroad then there is a credit on the current account. There is no question that the significant inflow of foreign direct investment and foreign portfolio investment into the City of London has helped to finance the UK's current account deficit.

- Multinationals also tend to invest more than domestic firms, meaning that they tend to operate plants which have higher productivity levels. When domestic suppliers do business with demanding foreign owned companies, it in turn raises their standards, thus there should be 'spill over' effects in terms of higher productivity in the economy.

- Multinationals bring transfers of knowledge and production techniques, such as Japanese methods of production in the UK car industry.

There are, of course, counter arguments to the above, suggesting that the net benefit of inward FDI is limited. They include:

- Multinationals can be 'footloose', for example, many of the East Asian companies that invested in the North East of England in the 1980s and 1990s have since left.

- They may drive domestic firms out of business.

- The repatriation of profits to the home country will lead to an outflow of income from the current account in the long run, worsening the balance of payments situation.

The UK's recent record of attracting inward FDI has been impressive. In 1998 the UK attracted more foreign investment than any other country in the world except the United States. The UK is also one of the biggest recipients of FDI in the EU, accounting for around 25% of all EU inward investment. As Figure 3.6 shows, the US easily accounts for the largest share of UK inward FDI, although that figure has declined from 34.4% in 2000 to 26.6% in 2007.

---

3. A lasting interest means an 'effective voice' in the company, i.e. ownership of 10% or more of the shares in the company.

Figure 3.6: Who invests in the UK?

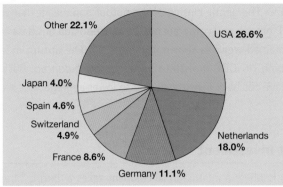

Source: ONS

Figure 3.7: Flows of UK inward net FDI

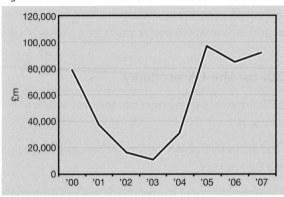

Source: ONS

Between 2001 and 2003, however, the rate of growth of inward FDI slowed significantly in the UK and the UK's share of EU FDI started to decline. At the time there was a global slowdown in FDI, due to the decline in cross border mergers and acquisitions that had led to the boom in global FDI in the late 1990s. The UK benefited disproportionately from the boom in mergers and acquisitions at the end of the 1990s as more of Britain's companies are publicly quoted on the Stock Exchange than elsewhere: the market for corporate control is more open than other parts of Europe, such as France. In any case, the effect of the fall in the share of FDI is somewhat muted, as it is the *absolute value* of the investment that affects the economy, not the *share*. FDI into the UK rebounded in 2004, and remained buoyant in 2005-7 (Figure 3.7). Although the figures for 2008-9 have not yet been published, it is likely that inward net FDI into the UK will have declined.

Questions

4. Explain two possible reasons why the US accounts for the largest share of inward UK FDI.

5. Evaluate the impact of inward FDI on the UK economy.

● Analysis: Why is the UK relatively attractive to foreign investors?

- A stable macroeconomic environment, at least until 2008
- A highly-skilled labour force, especially in financial services and certain high value added manufactures
- A relatively lightly regulated labour market
- The UK is a member of the European Single Market. This has led to non EU companies investing in the UK in order to avoid tariff and non-tariff barriers, as well as plenty of intra EU investment. In 2007, 50% of the *stock* of FDI in the UK was from the EU, up from 46.5% in 2000.

● Analysis: Possible threats to continuing inward FDI

- Some commentators believed that the reason for the decline in FDI in 2001-3 was the UK's decision not to join the euro. It may be that in future as more and more countries join and the UK stays out, FDI to the UK could decline.
- Government regulation on UK businesses has increased since 1997. This tends to affect small and medium sized firms disproportionately, whose owners have to deal with the so called 'red tape' as well as run the business.
- The higher tax burden has also arguably made the UK a slightly less attractive place to do business, despite the cuts in the headline rate of corporation tax made at the end of the 1990s and again in 2007.
- The credit crunch and subsequent recession of 2008-9 may have led to an outflow of FDI especially from the financial services industry.

Figure 3.8: Where do UK companies invest?

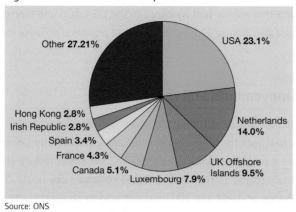

Source: ONS

It should also be noted that the UK is also a significant source of *outward* FDI to other economies. Figure 3.8 shows the *stock* of UK FDI. The largest single recipient of FDI from the UK is, unsurprisingly, the United States, with 23.1%. However, when all the members of the EU are added together the EU accounted for 42% of all of the stock of outward FDI from the UK in the global economy in 2007. Over the last ten years, the stock of UK outward FDI has increased steadily, only falling twice, during the global slowdown of 2001, and again to a lesser extent in 2004. A buoyant world economy saw UK FDI abroad rise steadily in 2005-6 and by 24% in 2007.

● Knowledge: The UK stock market

When share prices are rising on the stock exchange, the situation is known as a **bull market**. Around 25% of UK households own shares, so rising share prices lead to a rise in consumer wealth. When the price of shares rises, there is a **wealth effect**. Households may feel wealthier, so they feel able to spend more, or they may sell some of their shares and spend the proceeds. Either way, confidence rises, and there is a rise in consumer spending. In contrast, if share prices fall there may be a negative wealth effect, consumer confidence will fall, and consumer spending may decline. This is known as a **bear market**.

The actual price of shares on the stock exchange has no direct effect on companies' profits. This is because the stock exchange is a second-hand market. However, a fall in a company's share price may make it more susceptible to a takeover bid.

The price of a company's shares is determined by the demand for and supply of shares on the market. The willingness of shareholders to buy shares in a given company will be determined by the dividends that shareholders expect to receive on those shares, which in turn will be affected by the expected future profitability of the company. It will also be affected by the return on substitute assets, such as government bonds. So, ceteris paribus, share prices should go up when corporate profitability is expected to go up. Sometimes, however, the markets become over exuberant and share prices increase way beyond the present value of expected future dividends. This is known as a **bubble**. (The same thing, incidentally, has occurred in the UK housing market, see Chapter 2.)

● ● Application and Analysis: The 1997-2000 bull market

Figure 3.9: FTSE 100 Index (31 Dec 1983 = 100), month end

Source: www.wrenresearch.com

Figure 3.9 illustrates the bull market of 1997-2000. The stock market became overvalued thanks to a huge boom in technology stocks. Stock prices in technology, media and telecommunications companies increased well beyond what would have been predicted by profits actually generated. When this became obvious in 2000, a massive selling of shares began and the stock market collapsed.

As Figure 3.9 shows clearly, from 2003-2007 another bull market began, which lasted until the summer of 2007. In the middle of August

2007, however, the stock market got the jitters again, and there was a mini collapse in share prices. The trigger for this was the realisation that money lent by banks in the US sub-prime mortgage market would be unlikely to ever get paid back (see Chapter 1). This precipitated a general collapse in confidence, and a fall in stock markets worldwide.

● Evaluation: Stock market movements and recession

Around 25% of UK households own shares, although for many people their shareholdings constitute a small percentage of their financial wealth. Most shares in UK plcs are held by UK pension funds and insurance companies. Therefore a prolonged fall in the stock market could reduce the size of people's pensions. However, recent history suggests that stock market collapses are rarely closely followed by recessions. The stock market crashes of 1987 and 2001 did not lead to recession in the UK, for example. Therefore the size of this wealth effect is likely to be relatively small. However, business and consumer confidence can and did collapse after 2007. To the extent that they affect consumption and investment, a decline in the stock market could lead to a decline in UK GDP growth. However, it was not the main reason for the UK going into recession in 2008-9 (see Chapter 1). The stock market resumed an upward trend in 2009, even though the economy was still in recession.

●● Knowledge and Application: UK mergers and competition policy

The past ten years have seen two booms in mergers and acquisitions activity. Mergers and acquisitions tend to be highly *pro-cyclical*: when the UK and global economies are growing strongly, there tends to be a swelling of mergers and acquisitions activity. Strong economic growth in the UK and abroad, together with high business confidence and profitability, led to the boom in M&A activity both at home and abroad in the late 1990s as shown in Figures 3.10 and 3.11. There was an even larger boom from 2002-2007 but one of the differences between the new boom and the previous one in the 1990s was the number of companies bought by **private equity firms**. In 2006 and 2007, many UK plcs became the target of private equity companies with perhaps the most high profile example being the takeover of Alliance Boots by KKR. Boots had previously merged with Alliance Unichem, a healthcare distribution company, to form Alliance Boots in 2006.

Figure 3.10: Mergers in the UK by overseas companies

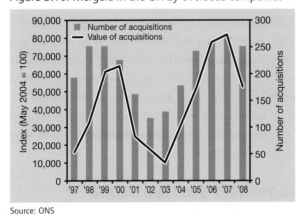

Source: ONS

Figure 3.11: Mergers abroad by UK companies

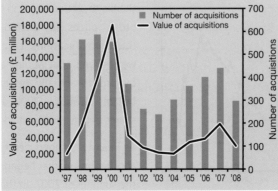

Source: ONS

Private equity firms are private companies or partnerships that borrow money to buy out the shareholders of a public limited company. Borrowing money to buy out the shareholders of a plc is known as a **leveraged buy out**. Private equity bosses argue that they will run a company more efficiently than when it was a plc, since the private equity firm is not accountable to a large number of shareholders, they will be less tempted to maximise short term shareholder profit and will look after the long term interests of the company. Critics, however, argue that rationalisation may create higher unemployment, and that private equity groups generally lead to greater indebtedness of the companies that they take over, particularly if interest rates increase, as they have in 2006 and 2007.

UK competition policy has been closely modelled on that of the EU. Chapter 1 of the 1998 Competition Act prohibits anti competitive agreements and restrictive practices by firms, while Chapter 2 of the Act prohibits the abuse of a dominant position in the UK market. The Competition Commission investigates monopolies and mergers inquiries and it also acts as an appeals tribunal, hearing appeals against decisions and penalties imposed by the DGFT pertaining to Chapter 1 and 2 infringement. A merger or takeover will be investigated by the DGFT if the combined market share of the firms involved is 25% or more, or where the value of the assets concerned exceeds £75 million. If the DGFT feels there are real competition issues to be addressed then he refers the case to the Competition Commission. Before 2002, the Secretary of State for Trade and Industry had the power of veto over referrals, and could make referrals on his/her own initiative, although in practice both were very rare. The Competition Commission could not conduct enquiries on its own initiative.

The 1998 Competition Act also substantially enhanced the powers of the Office of Fair Trading (OFT). As with the EU, the DGFT can authorise entry of business' premises without warning, conduct interviews and demand or seize documents from businesses. If a firm is found guilty of infringing Chapters 1 or 2 then the OFT can fine it up to 10% of UK turnover for up to three years before the date of the end of the infringement.

The 2002 Enterprise Act established the OFT as an independent statutory body, with a Board, and the post of DGFT was abolished. Whereas before the 2002 Act, the Secretary of State had to approve any referrals by the OFT to the Competition Commission: the OFT can now refer any proposal that it believes will curtail competition. Under the 2002 Act, the OFT and the Competition Commission now have the final say over whether mergers are anti competitive or not. Also the Competition Commission's previous role was only to make recommendations to the Secretary of State. Today the Secretary of State's role is substantially reduced: (s)he can only intervene in cases which raise exceptional public interest issues, e.g. involving mergers in the media sector or national security. The £75 million assets test outlined above has been replaced by a £70 million turnover test for determining whether mergers require investigation. Further, the old 'public interest' test has been replaced with a 'substantial lessening of competition' test, bringing UK competition policy closer to that of the American system. The organisation of cartels has now become a criminal offence and company directors can be jailed for up to five years. The parties involved have the right to apply to the Competitions Appeal Tribunal for a statutory judicial review of any decision of the OFT or Competition Commission. The hope is that the tougher legislation will act alongside that of the 1998 Competition Act to deter firms from entering into collusive agreements. In short, the 2002 Enterprise Act has effectively depersonalised and depoliticised UK competition policy, whereas previously Ministers found their involvement in matters like merger referrals regularly the subject of controversy. Nonetheless in a rare use of intervention by the government in September 2008 there was criticism of it for allowing Lloyds Bank to take over Halifax Bank of Scotland (HBOS) when this merger clearly resulted in a substantial lessening of competition in the market for house mortgages. In this case the OFT could not refer the merger to the Competition Commission. Subsequent to the merger it emerged that HBOS's mortgage business was full of bad debts – this at the height of the credit crunch (see Chapter 1) and this contributed significantly to the already weak position of Lloyds. But the story does not end there as the European Commission has sought for divestment by Lloyds (and also the Royal Bank of Scotland) following receipt of massive government help to avoid the collapse in the banking industry.

Chapter 4

Living Standards, Poverty and Inequality

This Chapter discusses how living standards changed during the past decade. It includes coverage of various measures of economic welfare before examining data measuring income inequality in the UK. This is followed by discussion of government policies to address inequality and work poverty and concludes with some data on regional differences in welfare within the UK.

● Knowledge: The standard of living

There is considerable debate amongst economists as to how to measure trends in living standards because the phrase 'standard of living' means different things to different people. Generally, economists use **income**, although expenditure and wealth are sometimes used. **Income** is defined as a **flow** of earnings, either in cash or in kind, from the employment of factors of production.

● Application: Rising living standards in the last decade

Figure 4.1: Growth in UK real household disposable income (2005 prices)

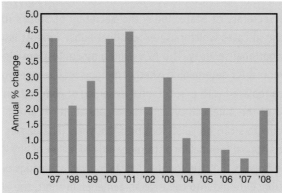

Source: ONS

For most people in the UK, living standards have increased in the last ten years. Between 1994/5 and 2007/8, low, medium and high income groups experienced a rise in real incomes before and after housing costs. The increase in UK average real income over this period was 29% before housing costs. However, since the early 2000s, real disposable income growth has been low compared to the boom years of the late 1990s, while mean and median income growth have slowed throughout Labour's three terms in office as shown in Figure 4.1 and Table 4.1.

Table 4.1: Annualised real average income growth (before housing costs) across parliaments, %

Government	Mean	Median
Conservative (Thatcher) 1979-1990	2.8	2.1
Conservative (Major) 1990-96/7	0.8	1.6
Labour 1996/7-2000/1	3.1	2.4
Labour 2000/1-2004/5	1.7	2.0
Labour 2004/5-2007/8	1.1	0.5

Source: M. Brewer, A. Muriel et al, *Poverty and Inequality in the UK 2009*, IFS

As far as the overall economy is concerned, the economist's benchmark measure of the standard of living is real GDP per capita. However, there are limitations of using the GDP figure as a guide to measuring living standards. These include:

- GDP is calculated using data from millions of different tax returns. There are bound to be accounting errors when dealing with so much information.

- The significance of the **underground economy**, e.g. illegal activities such as drugs and prostitution, or cash transactions that are not declared to the tax authorities. The Institute for Fiscal Studies (IFS) has estimated that the size of the UK underground or 'shadow' economy is £124 billion, a sum equivalent to 13% of GDP of the formal economy.

- Non-marketed items: if you baby-sit for a family, or if you redecorate your living room, it will not be recorded in the GDP statistics.

- The aggregate GDP figures do not show the *distribution of income* and wealth. In the UK there are significant variations in income and spending. Within each region there are pockets of prosperity as well as areas of high unemployment

- No account is taken of **externalities**: if growth is accompanied by pollution and congestion then the GDP figures will overstate the standard of living

- Nothing is revealed about the balance between consumption and investment – consumer-driven growth today may crowd out resources needed for investment, hampering long run development. UK growth was particularly unbalanced between 1997 and 2007 as noted in Chapter 1.

- GDP figures do not pick up improvements in the *quality* of goods and services. For example, cars are cheaper and of better quality than eighty years ago, but this would be reflected in a *reduction* in the GDP figure!

- There may be an opportunity cost associated with the rising value of national output: what about the *leisure time* foregone? If workers are working longer hours and generating more income, GDP rises, but living standards may not if people are losing valued leisure time

- GDP at market prices is calculated as $C + I + G + (X - M)$. This means a rise in the value of exports increases living standards, while a rise in the value of imports decreases living standards. This is overly simplistic and highly contentious. British consumers may not gain directly from firms concentrating on overseas markets, while our standard of living surely increases if we import a greater quantity of, say, oranges and bananas that we cannot grow ourselves.

- It could be argued that *intangible investments*, such as R&D in science, non-scientific R&D such as in design and financial services, and expenditure devoted to advertising, market research and training, that firms use to support their brands and organisational skills, should also be included in the GDP figures. At present they are not, but if they were included it would add significantly to GDP.

Exam hint

Bear in mind that at A level, you may well be asked to explain just two or three reasons why GDP data has limitations in detail. *Don't* just list factors: pick the ones that you feel most comfortable with, and explore and *analyse* them. Any data you have to back up your argument will doubtless impress the examiner!

Alternative measures to income

We consider the Index of Sustainable Economic Welfare and the UN Human Development Index before summarising some recent UK government indicators of the quality of life.

The ISEW (Index of Sustainable Economic Welfare) is an alternative composite indicator of living standards. It makes adjustments to account for factors that GDP ignores, such as:
- Inequality.
- Household production such as child care.

- 'Defensive' expenditures on health and education such as asthma treatment.
- Economic 'bads' such as commuting costs and car accidents.
- Environmental costs such as noise, air and water pollution and resource depletion and damage.

Between 1973 and 1996, UK GDP per capita rose by nearly 50% but the ISEW fell by over 13%. Although income per capita in the UK has risen during this period, inequality has risen, the environment has become more damaged and polluted and our lives more stressful. Thus the ISEW could be argued to be an improvement on GDP as it accounts for many of the factors mentioned above that GDP doesn't. However, the measurement of the amount of global warming and the damage caused by it is clearly imprecise and subject to fierce debate.

The United Nations began publishing the **Human Development Index** (HDI) in 1990. This is composed of three indicators, for which each country is given a score between 0 and 1. The HDI is a simple average of the three indices. They are:

- Real GDP per capita at PPP exchange rates.
- Life expectancy.
- Educational attainment, calculated by taking a weighted average of primary and secondary school enrolment rates and adult literacy.

A selection of HDI data is given in Table 4.2. For each country its ranking of GDP per capita rank minus its HDI ranking is one way of seeing whether the benefits of higher incomes are translated into quality of life. For example, Botswana's figure of -69 is because it has a relatively high GDP per capita, but a very low life expectancy because of the prevalence of AIDS. In contrast, Cuba's figure of +40 reflects Castro's National Literacy campaign, which gives it a relatively high HDI figure. Cuba's GDP figure is quite low, however, as Cuba is a command economy and therefore not run as efficiently as a market economy. The UK is ranked only one place lower on GDP per capita than on HDI.

The Index of Sustainable Economic Welfare makes adjustments for environmental costs such as pollution.

Table 4.2: HDI data, selected countries, 2006

Country	HDI Score	HDI Ranking	GDP per Capita (US $ PPP)	GDP per Capita Ranking	GDP per Capita – HDI Ranking
Iceland	0.968	1	35,814	14	13
Canada	0.967	3	36,687	12	9
Japan	0.956	8	31,951	24	16
France	0.955	11	31,980	23	12
United States	0.950	15	43,968	8	-7
United Kingdom	0.942	21	32,654	22	1
Cuba	0.855	48	6,876	88	40
China	0.762	94	4,682	104	10
Botswana	0.664	126	12,744	195	-69
India	0.609	132	2,489	126	-6

Source: UN website http://hdr.undp.org/en/statistics/data/

Evaluation of HDI as an indicator of living standards

Advantages	Disadvantages
Good composite indicator: tells us more than just the GDP per capita figure, and accounts for the fact that health and education are key development goals.	Weightings are arbitrary (i.e. random: reason for equal weightings not explained).
Used not as a dry statistical indicator, but as a tool to drive the development agenda.	It is an aggregate – like all aggregates, it hides the distribution.
Provides a better idea of well-being than GDP can.	Aggregates do not tell us why HDI may have changed over time.
The UN has begun to calculate disaggregated HDIs to distinguish between men and women, different regions and different ethnic groups: and thus avoid an aggregation problem.	Should quality of years lived be more important than the number?
Not so many indices to cause significant overlap,e.g. the infant mortality rate is not included but life expectancy is a key part of the HDI score.	Should it be quality of schooling, not just enrolment rates?
	May overstate development in countries with high inequality, e.g. Brazil: needs to be used in conjunction with other measures.

In 1998, the government introduced 13 new headline indicators of quality of life: economic growth, social investment, employment, health, education and training, housing quality, climate change, air pollution, transport, water quality, wildlife, land use and waste. More recently the Office for National Statistics has been exploring **social wellbeing** in the UK beyond economic growth. Social wellbeing includes:

(i) Involvement in empowered communities: including feelings of self-esteem, crime, political liberty, attitude to government.

(ii) Supportive personal relationships: satisfaction with social life, satisfaction with leisure time.

(iii) Good health: mortality rates, suicide rates, alcohol consumption, neurotic disorders.

(iv) Financial security: income, unemployment and employment, economic activity and inactivity, debt.

(v) Rewarding employment: educational achievement, level and quality of training and skills, job satisfaction.

(vi) A healthy and attractive environment: greenhouse gas and CO_2 emissions, energy consumption, river quality, biodiversity, attitude to waste management and recycling.

Question

1. Between 1992 and 2008 the UK experienced 16 years of uninterrupted economic growth. Examine the view this led to a higher standard of living in the UK.

We turn next to the subject of income inequality.

● ● Knowledge and Application: Measuring inequality in the UK

Figure 4.2: Real income growth by quintile group 1996/7 - 2007/8 (before housing costts)

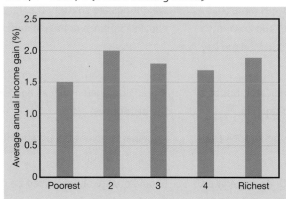

Source: M. Brewer, A. Muriel et al, *Poverty and Inequality in the UK 2009*, IFS

Figure 4.3: The UK Lorenz curve, various years

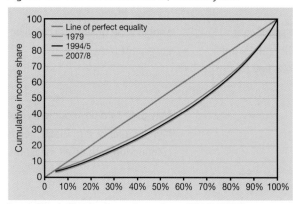

Source: Households Below Average Income Survey 1994/5-2007/8, www.dwp.gov.uk, A. Goodman and S. Webb, *For Richer, For Poorer: The Changing Distribution of Income in the United Kingdom 1961-1991*, IFS, 2009.

A note of caution re the 1979 data which is at 1994 prices, while the 1994/5 and 2007/8 data is at 2007/8 prices. However, the graph at least gives an idea of what has happened to the UK Lorenz curve. The median value for each decile is taken as the data point.

One way in which income inequality can be measured is to split the population into fifths or quintiles based on the level of real income earned. The poorest quintile is the poorest 20% of the population; the second quintile is the next 20% of income earners and so on until the fifth quintile is the richest 20% of the population. Figure 4.2 depicts the income growth by quintile during the Labour years. Under Labour, real income increased by more than under the Conservatives for all quintiles other than the richest quintile. Between 1996/97 and 2007/08 the second quintile clearly experienced the highest annual real income growth at 2.0%. Figure 4.2 suggests very little change in income inequality under Labour, which is in stark contrast to the Conservative era, when the highest quintile of income earners experienced the highest real income growth, followed by the fourth, third, second and poorest in that order.

However, Figure 4.2 only considers 5 percentile points in the entire income distribution. The **Lorenz curve** provides a diagrammatic and more comprehensive representation of inequality as shown in Figure 4.3. The x axis shows the cumulative percentage of the population and the y axis the cumulative share of equivalised income.

We split the cumulative population shares into ten, so the first data point is the income share of the poorest 10% of the population, the second the poorest 20% and so on. The term 'equivalised' means that the figure for disposable income for each household has been adjusted to take into account different household size and composition. The green 45 degree line is the line of perfect equality, which is what the Lorenz curve would look like if each decile earned exactly 10% of the income, i.e. if there was no inequality. Figure 4.3 makes clear that the Lorenz curve for 1994/5 lies further to the right at every data point than that of 1979, revealing that income inequality in the UK must have increased over this time period. However, there is very little difference between the Lorenz curves for 1994/5 and for 2007/8 and it is rather imprecise to compare simply by eye! So the Lorenz curve is limited in what it can tell us about inequality in different years.

The Lorenz curve is useful, however, in that it enables us to obtain a more accurate summary measure of inequality: the **Gini coefficient**. This figure is more appropriate as it takes account of the entire income distribution. The Gini coefficient is the ratio of the area enclosed between the Lorenz curve and the 45 degree line to the total area underneath the 45 degree line.

Question

2. Explain how economists might compare the level of inequality across different countries.

●● Application and Analysis: Gini coefficient system

Figure 4.4 indicates that inequality as measured by the Gini coefficient increased significantly in the mid to late 1980s. This reflects more rapid growth at the top of the income distribution that that at the bottom as noted above. But we can offer several underlying reasons for greater inequality:

Figure 4.4: The Gini coefficient

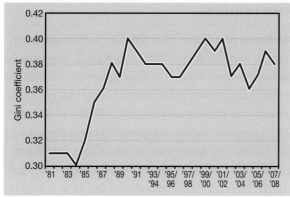

Source: ONS, 'The effects of taxes and benefits on household income, 2007/08'. The figures for the Gini coefficient are for post tax equivalised income.

Figure 4.5: The 90/10 ratio

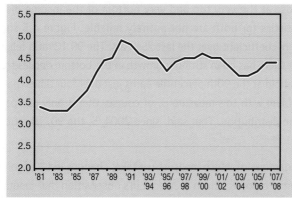

Source: ONS, 'The effects of taxes and benefits on household income, 2007/08'.

(i) A sharp rise in earnings inequality, due to falling demand for unskilled and semi-skilled labour and rising demand for skilled labour. Technological change has reduced demand for repetitive jobs in sectors such as architecture and engineering. Innovation has advanced more quickly than workers' ability to embody the new skills. The demand for skilled workers has thus expanded quicker than supply, raising the premium received by skilled workers.

(ii) A sharp rise in the number of individuals of working age living in workless households, largely down to declining male participation, in turn linked to structural unemployment.

(iii) A rise in female participation amongst those households with working partners. This led to a polarisation between no earner and two-earner households.

(iv) The number of self-employed individuals increased hugely in the 1980s. Since differences in earnings amongst the self-employed are greater than for the earnings distribution as a whole, so earnings inequality rose.

(v) The decision in 1981 to increase benefit levels in line with inflation rather than with earnings led to an increase in the earnings gap between those living on benefits and those in work.

(vi) Government policies to reduce trade union power and abolish minimum wage protection in certain industries widened the pay gap between the low paid and the rest of the labour force.

(vii) Tax changes such as the switch from direct to indirect taxation and the cuts in the top rate of income tax (see Chapter 10) also widened income distribution.

Over the period 1990-96, income inequality as measured by the Gini coefficient fell, but only slightly, and nowhere near far enough to reverse the rapid increase of the 1980s. Reasons include:

• Slower growth in employment income compared to the mid to late 1980s. During periods of economic growth, middle and high income earners tend to gain the most, pulling away from low income households. This effect was less pronounced during the recession and recovery of 1990-96.

• The increases in direct taxation in the early 1990s.

• The rise in means-tested benefits in the early 1990s.

From 1995/6-2001/2, income inequality rose slightly, but then fell back again until 2004/5, because of:

• Faster growth in earnings at the bottom of the distribution.

• Faster growth in self-employment income at the bottom of the distribution.

• Increases in the minimum wage and tax credits.

• The rise in NICs in 2003.

Extension material: What can we conclude

If we just consider the part of the income distribution from the 20th to 85th percentile, then the lower the income, the higher the income growth over the period 1996/7 to 2007/8. This indicates falling inequality over this portion of the distribution. However, above the 85th percentile, income growth is higher, the higher the income. This could be due to large salary increases and bonuses for executives of big companies, and the effects of the cut in the top rate of income taxes in the 1980s, which has allowed the rich to accumulate capital. Below the 20th percentile, the income growth is lower, the lower the income, and real income growth has been negative for the very lowest part of the income distribution. *Taking the income distribution as a whole, then, inequality has hardly changed at all.* It has fallen over most of the distribution, but this has been counteracted by the fact that income growth has been low or negative at the bottom of the distribution, and rapid at the top of the distribution.

The 90:10 ratio is another summary measure of inequality. It is simply the disposable income of the household at the 90th percentile expressed as a ratio of the household at the 10th percentile. It is a useful measure in that it excludes those at the very top and very bottom of the income distribution which is convenient given that the statistics for both are not entirely reliable. Figure 4.5 shows that this has followed a similar path to the Gini coefficient over the last 25 years. The 90:10 ratio fell between 1999/00 and 2004/5 due to the fact that there has been stronger growth in the bottom deciles than the top deciles in recent years. Today, the household at the 90th percentile earns just over four times that of the household at the 10th percentile. The problem with this measure is, of course, that it only compares households at two points in the overall income distribution. That said, since 2004/5, the 90/10 ratio has risen slightly again.

Overall, it would appear that regardless of which measure we take, changes in UK income inequality have been fairly mild since Labour came to power. Given Brewer et al's observation that inequality is falling over the distribution between the 20th and 85th percentiles, very strong growth at the top of the distribution and low growth at the bottom (negative for the lowest percentile) has driven the very slight rise in inequality. Having said this, it is more the *level* of the Gini coefficient, around 0.38 today, that is the cause for concern, this is much higher than most of the post war period.

● Knowledge: The case for and against inequality

Free market economists would point out that wage inequality is necessary for the efficient functioning of a market-based economy. Differences in wages create the incentive for workers to work harder: if a worker's wage is based on his productivity, then he will work hard in order to gain a high wage. If wage differentials are very narrow, for example due to excessive trade union power or high minimum wages, and have less to do with the productivity of the workers, then work effort will be lower and the economy will not run efficiently.

Critics of free market economists such as Dugger argue that inequality is a systematic division of society into groups, for the benefit of one group at the harm of another.[1] Inequality involves a systematic suppression of groups in society, creating jealousies and social instability. The result could be rising crime rates and other negative externalities, which ultimately damage the performance of the economy.

Question

3. To what extent is the current degree of inequality of income in the UK harmful to the economy?

The evidence that inequality has not fallen significantly since 1997 may seem surprising given Labour's efforts to redistribute income. The tax and benefit system in the UK is redistributive in nature. The post tax and benefit distribution of income is more equal than the pre tax and benefit distribution. Table 4.2 shows how this is brought about.

Table 4.3: The redistributive nature of government

Original Income (Wages and Salaries, Self Employment Income, Pensions, Investment Income)

+ Cash Benefits

= **Gross Income**

− Direct Taxes and NICs

= **Disposable Income**

− Indirect Taxes

= **Post Tax Income**

+ Benefits in kind (Education, NHS)

= **Final Income**

	Gross Income	Disposable Income	Post Tax Income	Final Income
Gini Coefficient 2007/8	0.52	0.38	0.34	0.38

Most direct taxes are **progressive**. This means that as income rises, the proportion of income taken in tax also rises. Indirect taxes are **regressive**: as income rises, the proportion of income paid in tax falls. The government can alter the post tax distribution of income by altering the mix between direct and indirect taxation. In addition, the government can alleviate poverty and inequality by increasing benefits. Some of

1. W. Dugger, 'Against Inequality', *Journal of Economic Issues*, June 1998.

these benefits are **universal**, such as the state pension and child benefit, while others are **means tested**, such as income support.

Question

4. The best way to reduce inequality is through redistributive policies. To what extent do you agree with this statement?

●● Analysis and Evaluation:
Government policies to tackle inequality and in work poverty

Several policies have been introduced to address inequality and we now summarise these.

(i) The introduction of a National Minimum Wage

The NMW was introduced in 1999 and since then the government has increased it above the rate of growth of average earnings. The rate for workers aged 22 and over stands at £5.80/hour as of October 2009. The rate for 18-21 year olds is £4.83/hour and the rate for 16-17 year olds is £3.57 per hour. Proponents of the minimum wage argue that it has reduced in work poverty and helped to prevent the exploitation of the low-paid workforce. It has helped to boost work incentives, since a rise in the pay floor increases the opportunity cost of an hour of leisure. The introduction of the NMW does not appear to have increased the level of unemployment in the UK economy.

Critics of the national minimum wage argue that it does not take into account differences in the regional cost of living. Thus in 2007, London citizens were advocating a minimum wage of £7.05/hour for London to account for the exceedingly high cost of living there. Neither is it enough on its own to achieve the degree of redistribution that the Labour government wishes.

(ii) New Working Families and Children's Tax Credits in 1999

These were top up benefits paid to low income workers with families through the pay packet again introduced in 1999. They were replaced in 2003 by the Working Tax Credit and the Child Tax Credit, which are paid directly into your bank account. To be eligible for working tax credit, people without children must be 25 or over and work at least 30 hours per week. People with children must work at least 16 hours per week, and if you have children and you work 30 hours a week or more, you get an additional amount. Relief is reduced by 37p in the pound above a threshold amount.

The case for these tax credits is that they improve the incentive to work by reducing the **poverty trap**. The poverty trap is the situation where if you are on a low income, and your income rises, you are often no better or even worse off in terms of disposable income: as your income rises, the amount of money you can claim in benefits falls, while the tax you owe increases. The aim of the tax credits is to reduce the financial disincentive to work so that your effective marginal income tax rate is lower than it would have been without the tax credits.

However tax credits as a means of redistributing income and boosting the incentive to work are not without problems.

- By reducing the rate at which benefits taper off, it provides benefit to those families in the 'withdrawal zone', i.e. those who are earning above the threshold, who may now have less incentive to take better jobs or work longer hours.

- They worsen the government's finances in the short term, increasing the PSNB.

- They are complex! This has meant that many of those who are eligible for tax credits have not claimed them. It has also meant that HM Revenue and Customs has miscalculated the tax credit and by 2007 it had overpaid claimants by £6bn since the 2003 launch. In addition, the tax credit system has been subject to fraud. In 2005, the online tax credit portal was closed after a sustained attack by fraudsters.

- The introduction of a new 10p starting rate of income tax in 2000-01. In the Budget of 2007, Gordon Brown announced a 2p cut in the basic rate of income tax to 20%. However, the 10p starting rate was abolished in 2008.

- The New Deal programme, introduced in 1998, to combat long term unemployment (see Chapter 7).

- Increases in means-tested pension credit to reduce pensioner poverty.

The Institute of Fiscal Studies has found that tax and benefit changes since 1997 have been progressive in effect, i.e. they have benefited the less well off relative to the better off. Though the tax and benefit changes up until 2000/1 have had little effect, since then there has been a significant rise in means-tested benefits and tax credits. Therefore the government's tax and benefit policies have at least halted the growth in inequality, though they have not succeeded in their aim of reducing it. The increases in child tax credit from 2008-10, the new top rate of income tax from 2011, and the raising of the threshold from which workers start to pay National Insurance Contributions from 2011 should all reduce inequality in the future. However, rising unemployment, particularly amongst the less well educated, may increase inequality.

Question

5. Examine the effectiveness of three policies that could be used to reduce UK poverty.

Knowledge and Application: The distribution of wealth in the UK

Wealth is a **stock** concept, meaning that it is the ownership of assets valued at a particular point in time. Table 4.4 gives data on the ownership of marketable wealth in the UK economy. Marketable wealth includes physical wealth such as land, housing, and consumer durables such as cars, DVD players, widescreen TVs and also financial wealth such as shares and other financial assets. Non-marketable wealth includes mainly occupational and state pension rights. Wealth is generally far more unevenly distributed than income, as individuals accumulate assets over the course of their working life and then draw on them after they have retired, with others inheriting the remainder at the time of death. There is also a positive correlation with educational attainment and financial wealth net of debt. For individuals in Great Britain aged between 50 and 54, median net financial wealth was £23,000 for people with a degree, £13,000 for those with qualifications at a lower level and £1,500 for those with no qualifications. Since wealth generates income, wealth inequality will always be a cause of income inequality.

Table 4.4: Ownership of UK marketable wealth

Percentage of wealth owned by:	1991	1996	2001	2002	2003
Most wealthy 1%	17	20	22	24	21
Most wealthy 25%	71	74	72	75	72
Most wealthy 50%	92	92	94	94	93
Total marketable wealth (£bn)	1,711	2,092	3,477	3,588	3,783

Source: ONS, *Social Trends 37*

In 2003, the wealthiest 1 per cent owned just over a fifth of the UK's marketable wealth, while half the population shared only 7 per cent of total marketable wealth. Note, however, that over time changes in the distribution of wealth have been much less drastic than changes in inequality, although wealth inequality has risen slightly since 1996.

Question

6. Explain, in your own words, the difference between wealth and income.

Extension material: Inheritance tax

In 2007, the major political parties engaged in debate over inheritance tax. Inheritance tax is levied at 40% on the value of assets worth more than £312,000 when someone dies, unless it is left to your spouse. In October 2007 the Chancellor raised the tax threshold for married couples to £600,000. The Conservatives suggested the threshold should be raised to £1 million. Critics of inheritance tax have argued that as property prices have risen so rapidly, more and more people, not necessarily rich people, have been dragged into paying inheritance tax, particularly since Gordon Brown did not raise the threshold significantly during his ten years as Chancellor. Others argue that it is one of the few remaining progressive tax measures left, and it should not just be paid by the super rich.

● Knowledge: Poverty definitions

Poverty is a *normative* concept: one person's interpretation of what poverty means may be different to that of another. Therefore it is very hard to define.

Absolute poverty may be 'a situation in which an individual, household or society is unable to access the basic needs for survival, such as food, air to breathe, clean water and shelter'.

Relative poverty is poverty relative to a comparator group. The UK government measures relative poverty by measuring the proportion of the population below various proportions of median income. These proportions are known as **poverty lines**. The government uses 60% of median income as the measure of the poverty line in its annual poverty audit, and it is this measure that is used here.

● ● Application and Analysis: Changes in poverty since 1997

Relative poverty fell in the UK during Labour's first two terms for children, pensioners and all people regardless of whether income is measured before or after housing costs as shown in Tables 4.5 and 4.6. Initiatives such as Working Families Tax Credit, the Children's Tax Credit, and more generous means-tested benefit for pensioners contributed to the fall in relative poverty. However, during Labour's third term so far, relative poverty increased on each measure from the corresponding values in 2004/5. This came as a disappointment to a Labour government that had placed reduction of relative poverty as one of its key aims.

Table 4.5: Relative poverty in the UK: households below 60% of median income (after housing costs, AHC)

	Children (%)	Children (millions)	Pensioners (%)	Pensioners (millions)	All (%)	All (millions)
1996/97	34.1	4.3	29.1	2.9	25.3	14.0
2000/01	31.1	3.9	25.9	2.6	23.1	13.0
2004/05	28.4	3.6	17.6	1.9	20.5	12.1
2007/8	31.1	4.0	18.1	2.0	22.5	13.5

Source: A. Goodman and S. Webb, *For Richer, For Poorer: The Changing Distribution of Income in the United Kingdom 1961-1991*, IFS, 2009

Table 4.6: Relative poverty in the UK: households below 60% of median income (before housing costs, BHC)

	Children (%)	Children (millions)	Pensioners (%)	Pensioners (millions)	All (%)	All (millions)
1996/97	26.7	3.4	24.6	2.4	19.4	10.8
2000/01	23.3	3.0	24.8	2.5	18.4	10.4
2004/05	21.3	2.7	21.3	2.3	17.0	10.0
2007/8	22.5	2.9	22.7	2.5	18.3	11.0

Source: A. Goodman and S. Webb, *For Richer, For Poorer: The Changing Distribution of Income in the United Kingdom 1961-1991*, IFS, 2009

Labour's policies to arrest poverty have been focused on redistributing income towards low income families with children and pensioners. The government had a target for child poverty in 2004/5 to be a quarter lower than its 1998/9 level. It missed this target by 100,000 on the BHC measure, and by 300,000 on the AHC measure. In 1999 the government also stated that they aimed to halve child poverty by 2010/11, and eliminate it altogether by 2020. The IFS project that by 2010 the target will be missed by 0.6 million on the BHC measure. However, the cut in basic income tax from 22% to 20% in 2008, rises in the point below which people pay Working Tax Credit, and increases in child tax credit above the growth of average earnings should help to help to reduce in work poverty for those with children.

The government have also measured trends in absolute poverty, by fixing the poverty lines in real terms at 60% of the 1996/7 median income. The IFS found that by 2004/5 AHC, child and pensioner poverty had more than halved, and poverty for the population as a whole had fallen by just under half. However, since then absolute child and pensioner poverty have increased from their 2004/5 levels AHC and BHC, while absolute poverty for all persons has risen for three consecutive years.

Of course, while the above evidence depicts falling rates of poverty on trend, it does not tell us anything about the *depth* of poverty of those who fall below the poverty line. This is measured by calculating the poverty gap, by taking how far the median poor individual falls short of the poverty line. On this measure, the poverty gap has remained constant for all groups, including pensioners, apart from children, where it has fallen slightly. This suggests that overall, while the number of people in poverty has fallen, poverty is becoming a more serious problem for those who are still experiencing it.

Question

7. (i) Explain why some individuals are in relative poverty in the UK.
   (ii) Examine the effect of redistributive policies on the level of relative poverty.

● ● Knowledge and Application: An economic divide across the regions

The aggregate UK figures for poverty and inequality commented on above disguise the fact that there are substantial inequalities between regions in the economy. **Regional policy** is designed to redistribute income to regions of below average economic performance. Such initiatives include:

• Regional Selective Assistance (RSA) – grants towards industrial projects.

• Regional Enterprise Grants (REGs) designed to assist small and medium sized enterprises.

• The European Regional Development Fund.

In the early 1990s, the divide between the regions narrowed, as the early 1990s recession hit the service based industries harder than manufacturing. However, it has since accelerated again. Figure 4.6 shows that only three regions experienced higher growth in gross value added (GVA) per head than the UK average: London, South East and Northern Ireland, while the largest decline was in Wales. The levels of the red bars provide strong evidence of a North-South divide in the economy.

In addition, the surge in house prices and the collapse in unemployment in the mid to late 1990s were more prominent in the South East and less so in the North East and North West, as structural unemployment persisted.

Figure 4.6: Gross Value Added per head across the regions

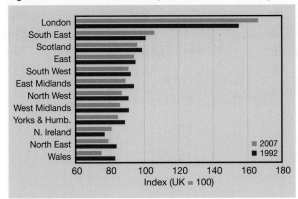

Source: ONS, *Regional Trends* 41 (2009)

Figure 4.7: Regional unemployment rates in March-May 2009

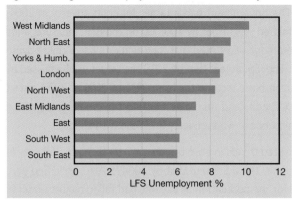

Source: ONS, *Regional Trends 41* (2009)

Figure 4.8: Average UK house price by region

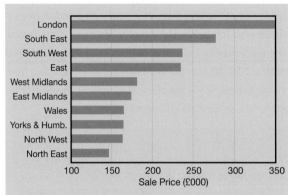

Source: ONS, *Regional Trends 41* (2009)

Between 2000 and 2007, however, house prices rose rapidly in the North East, employment and activity rates increased, and the Northern regions began to close the gap. Nevertheless, unemployment remains higher, and house prices substantially lower, in the northern regions.

Perhaps most stark is the situation in London. Figure 4.6 shows the much higher GVA per head and Figure 4.8 makes clear the much higher level of house prices than in all other regions. This has led some commentators to claim that there is less of a North-South divide in the UK as much as a London-Rest of the UK divide. However, London is not without its economic problems: activity rates are lower than anywhere else in England apart from the North East. Figure 4.7 shows that the unemployment rate is almost as high in London as it is in the North East and Yorkshire. Table 4.7 indicates that child poverty in the capital appears to be vast. This also helps to illustrate a more general point: that there is as much divide *within* regions as *between* regions in the UK.

Table 4.7: *Selected regional economic and social indicators 2008*

	% Children living in workless households	% Population of working age claiming a social security benefit	Economic Activity Rates %
North East	20	18.8	75.8
North West	18	17.4	77.0
Yorkshire & the Humber	16	14.9	77.8
East Midlands	13	13.4	79.9
West Midlands	19	15.7	77.2
East	12	11.1	81.3
London	23	13.6	76.8
South East	10	9.9	82.7
South West	13	11.7	81.6
Wales	16	18.6	76.4
Scotland	15	16.3	79.8
Northern Ireland	13	N/A	73.2

Source: ONS, *Regional Trends 41* (2009)

Chapter 5

UK Trade, the Current Account and the Value of the Pound

This Chapter explains the constituent parts of the UK's current Balance of Payments before looking closely at trends in the net position of trade in goods, trade in services and investment income. It then evaluates the significance of the UK's persistent deficit on current account. The Chapter ends considering the external value of the pound sterling including the effects of a strong sterling value of the pound and also of a weak pound.

● Knowledge: The meaning of the current account

The current account measures flows of income into and out of the economy. There are four main parts to the UK current account:

(a) The **balance of trade in goods**: for example oil, agricultural products, clothing, raw materials and machinery.

(b) The **balance of trade in services**: net income from shipping, insurance, finance, tourism, international transport and so on.

(c) The **income balance** is more complex. It is the balance of investment income, i.e. the net figure plus the balance of compensation of employees, again a net amount. Thus the investment income balance is income earned on UK assets located overseas minus the income earned from foreign-owned assets located in the UK. It includes the acquisition of foreign companies and investment in physical capital overseas, as well as portfolio investment, which includes buying shares. The second part of the income balance is the compensation of individuals which is the earnings made by people from economies other than those in which they are residents.

To put the above in more plain English, if Nissan sends profits generated from its Sunderland plant back to Japan, this is an *outflow* of investment income. If a BP employee in Azerbaijan sends money back to her family in the UK, this is one *inflow* in the transactions relating to compensation of individuals.

(d) **Net transfers** include foreign aid, the UK's contribution to the EU budget and funds brought by migrants to the UK.

Questions

1. Distinguish between a current account deficit and a budget deficit.

2. Explain the impact on the current account balance of the following:
    (i)   An American tourist spends money on a holiday to London.
    (ii) A UK pharmaceuticals company sells its hot lemon drinks to Germany.
    (iii) A French car company uses a UK shipping company.
    (iv) Vodafone sends its profits made in Sweden back to the UK.
    (v)   A Polish plumber based in the UK sends money home to Poland.
    (vi) The UK pays its subscription to the International Monetary Fund.

Question

3. The current account balance:

   A. is always in surplus when the value of imports exceeds the value of exports.

   B. goes into surplus whenever net transfers fall

   C. is in deficit whenever the government borrows money.

   D. includes trade in goods and services.

● Application: The state of the current account in 2008

One of the UK government's four macroeconomic objectives is to achieve current account equilibrium, that is, that inflows of income should equal outflows. Table 5.1 shows that this was very clearly not achieved in 2008!

Table 5.1: Summary of UK current account balance in 2008 (current, seasonally adjusted)

	£m
Export of goods	251,102
Import of goods	343,979
Export of services	170,399
Import of services	115,920
Balance of trade in goods and services	-38,398
Income Balance	26,940
Net transfers	-13,610
Current Account Balance	**-25,068**

Source: ONS, *UK Pink Book 2009*

Understanding international trade is vital to understanding the UK economy as a whole. The UK is one of the most open developed economies in the world. The value of UK exports and imports were each close to 30% of the value of UK GDP in 2008. The UK was also the second biggest exporter of commercial services and the eighth biggest exporter of goods in 2007. There has, however, been a serious decline in the competitiveness of the UK on trade in goods, and import penetration has risen. This has led to the UK running a persistent **current account deficit**.

Understanding international trade is vital to understanding the UK economy as a whole.

Figure 5.1: Top 10 UK export destinations 2008

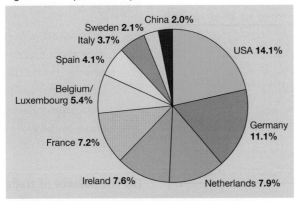

Source: ONS, *Monthly Review of External Trade Statistics*, June 2009

Figure 5.2: Top 10 UK import sources 2008

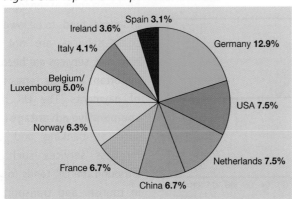

Source: ONS, *Monthly Review of External Trade Statistics*, June 2009

Figure 5.3: Top 10 UK exports by commodity 2008 (£m)

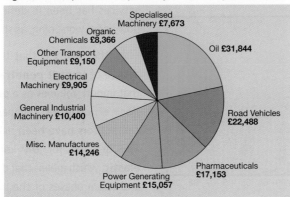

Source: ONS, *Monthly Review of External Trade Statistics*, June 2009

Figure 5.4: Top 10 UK imports by commodity 2008 (£m)

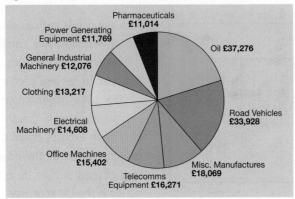

Source: ONS, *Monthly Review of External Trade Statistics*, June 2009

Despite globalisation, most countries still tend to do the majority of their trade with their neighbours. The UK is no exception. In 2008 the EU accounted for 56.2% of UK exported goods and 52.4% of UK imported goods. These proportions have risen substantially since the UK joined the EU back in 1973. However, the EU as a region has experienced sluggish economic growth in recent years. The share of UK trade with newly industrialising countries in Asia has risen slightly over the last twenty five years. However, it seems we are still not trading enough with faster growing nations. A report in *The Sunday Times* in August 2004 highlighted how the UK is so far doing very little trade with the fastest growing economies of the world, such as China and India. The United States remains the country to which we export the most in value terms: accounts for 14.1% of our exports in 2008 as shown in Figure 5.1. The UK buys more of its imports (12.9%) from Germany than from anywhere else as Figure 5.2 shows.

(a) The balance of trade in goods

In value terms, the most important goods traded between the UK economy and the rest of the world are oil, road vehicles, pharmaceuticals and telecommunications equipment. The main goods traded as exports are shown in Figure 5.3 and those imported in Figure 5.4. The UK has traditionally run a **deficit** on its balance of trade in goods. Figure 5.5 shows how this deficit has worsened over the last twelve years, although the deficit as a percentage of GDP has remained fairly constant and actually narrowed slightly in 2009. One important commodity that was until recently always in surplus, however, was the oil balance (Figure 5.6), which prevented the goods deficit from worsening still further. In the second quarter of 2005, however, the oil balance moved into deficit, where it has stayed for four years due to declining output from the North Sea as that source has now been almost fully exploited.

Figure 5.5: UK balance of trade in goods

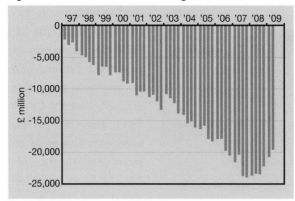

Source: ONS, *UK Pink Book*, June 2009

Figure 5.6: UK oil balance

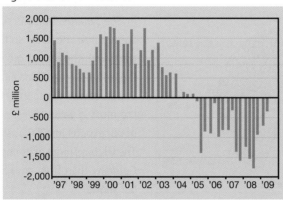

Source: ONS, *UK Pink Book*, June 2009

Figure 5.7: UK balance of trade in services

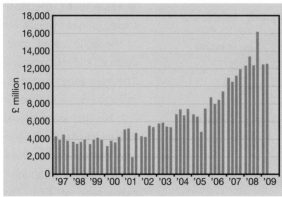

Source: ONS, *UK Pink Book*, June 2009

Figure 5.8: UK balance of trade in goods and services

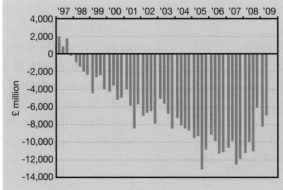

Source: ONS, *UK Pink Book*, June 2009

Question

4. Explain whether or not Figures 5.3-5.4 provide evidence that the UK economy trades on the basis of comparative advantage. (HINT: discuss **inter**-industry trade vs. **intra**-industry trade.

(b) The balance of trade in services

In contrast to the performance of trade in goods, Figure 5.7 indicates that the UK has a healthy surplus in services. The value of trade in services tends to be lower than in goods, as some services are not easily tradable. However, services are becoming increasingly important in value terms to the UK balance of payments. The UK has a substantial **comparative advantage** in financial services such as banking and professional and business services such as consultancy, although the UK tends to run a large deficit in tourism and transport. The surplus in services does not offset the deficit in goods, however, so the balance of trade in goods and services has been in deficit for some years now and is worsening, as shown in Figure 5.8.

The other worry is that the UK has a high degree of **import penetration**. This means that import volumes as a percentage of total final expenditure, compared to its major competitors have been rising. (Figure 5.9). The demand for UK imports is **income elastic**, which means that during the recovery and boom phases of the business cycle, the demand for imports rises more than proportionately. There is a particularly high degree of import penetration in manufactured goods such as electrical machinery, motor vehicles and computer and office machinery. The growth of UK import penetration has also been more rapid than all of the UK's major competitors with the exception of the US. Coupled with the relative decline in exports of UK manufactures, we can conclude that there has been a serious lack of, and decline in, competitiveness in goods in the UK economy.

Figure 5.9: UK import penetration

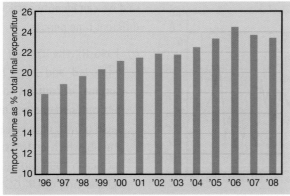

Source: OECD

Figure 5.10: UK net income balance

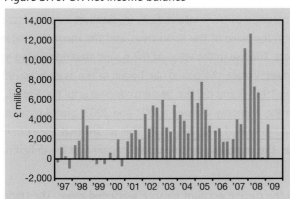

Source: ONS, *UK Pink Book*, June 2009

Figure 5.11: UK net transfers balance

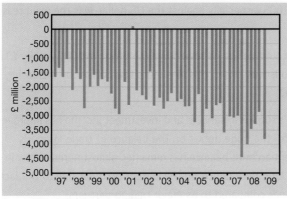

Source: ONS, *UK Pink Book*, June 2009

Question

5. Examine two possible reasons for growing UK import penetration.

(c) The income balance

The net investment income section of the current account tends to be in surplus, and has traded at a very healthy surplus in recent times as is clearly illustrated in Figure 5.10. The large net income balance between 2002 and 2006 reflects buoyant direct investment income when the world economy was growing strongly. But the balance fell in 2008, however, due to a fall in foreign earnings of banks and insurance companies, linked to the global financial crisis.

(d) Net transfers

The fourth and final part of the current account, net transfers is a relatively small component of the current account, and tends to be in deficit given the fact that the UK is a net contributor to the EU budget. The deficit has also worsened considerably in recent years as revealed in Figure 5.11.

● Analysis: The current account balance during the last decade

If we now add all four parts of the current account together for the years before 2008 what picture emerges? The trend in the overall current account balance is shown in Figure 5.12. The fluctuations in the current account balance tend to be **counter-cyclical**, that is they follow the opposite course to that of the economic cycle. During a recovery or upswing, demand for imports tends to increase as domestic capacity becomes constrained, while domestic firms tend to concentrate on the booming home market rather than selling abroad. Thus *the current account balance tends to deteriorate during an upturn*. Relatively strong domestic GDP growth from 1997-2007 has partly accounted for the deficit: as UK consumers have gained more income, they have spent some of this extra income on imports. During a slowdown or recession, domestic firms look to sell in faster-growing markets abroad, while demand for imports contracts due to

Figure 5.12: UK current account balance

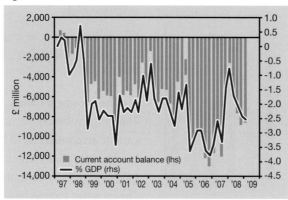

Source: ONS, *UK Pink Book*, June 2009

declining real incomes. These generalisations said we can identify particular factors in four different time periods.

(i) 1996-8: The current account balance improved and even briefly went into surplus, in contrast to the propositions just outlined above. This was because of rapid growth of overseas markets such as the US, which led to a surge in investment income in 1998 and exports of services. A rebalancing of UK GDP growth in 1998 towards investment also helped restrain the growth in imports.

(ii) 1999-2003: The current account was back into deficit. Investment income declined following the slowdown in global growth in the wake of the Asian crisis, and the rise in the value of the pound on the foreign exchange markets. The rise in the value of the pound sterling also led to a growing deficit in the balance of trade in goods. In fact, the pound had begun to rise as early as 1996, but the current account balance improved in 1997-8 and did not begin to decline until the end of 1998, indicating a **reverse J curve effect** for the economy. Between 2001 and 2003, global economic growth slowed, while the value of the pound remained relatively high. This meant that the current account balance remained in deficit. However, the improving income surplus meant that the deficit narrowed, as shown in Figure 5.12.

(iii) 2004-6: In this time period the current account balance worsened again. The trade in goods balance worsened, the service sector surplus briefly worsened and the oil balance went into a significant deficit for the first time. The income balance also fell in the third and fourth quarter of 2005. The increase in the value of the pound in 2006, especially against the US dollar, was the main reason why the deficit was so high.

(iv) 2007-2008: The current account deficit narrowed by £6.1 billion in 2007 and by £12.6 billion in 2008. Although the deficit in goods was larger, this was more than offset by increasing surpluses on both trade in services and income.

To summarise, although the UK's surplus in services and investment income has improved over the last ten years, it has failed to make up for the huge deficit on the balance of trade in goods. Despite fluctuations in the economic cycle, the current account balance has remained almost permanently in deficit. This shows that *the UK has a structural or long term deficit on the current account*, due to the lack of price and non price competitiveness of UK goods compared to its major trading partners.

So the main reasons for the UK current account deficit are:

• Strong growth in consumer spending, which has sucked in imports.

• A high value of the pound, which rose notably during 1996-2001 and 2006-7.

• A rise in import penetration, partly due to consumer spending, but also due to globalisation and the industrialisation of China, India and Latin American countries.

• Poor non-price competitiveness which means a lack of quality, poor design and reliability of UK goods. This has improved since the 1970s, but some research in the late 1990s suggests that the share of UK's total manufacture exports in the 'up market' unit value category were still below that of the EU average. This is despite a few successes such as pharmaceuticals, biotechnology and aerospace. Low productivity, high unit labour costs and low fixed capital investment help to explain the UK's lack of competitiveness (see below).

● Evaluation: Does the current account deficit matter?

At first glance, the deterioration in the current account balance below looks like a cause for concern, as the government is continually failing to meet one of its macroeconomic objectives. In the same way that an individual cannot spend more than she earns unless she runs down her savings or borrows, the economy cannot do the same without either borrowing from abroad or reducing its savings and investments abroad. However, the fact that the City of London has attracted such high levels of foreign direct investment and foreign portfolio investment has meant that there has been sufficient financial capital flowing into the UK economy to pay for the deficit. As long as this continues to occur, there is no reason why the UK cannot afford its trade deficit. That said, trends in global financial markets can be volatile, and it may be unwise to rely on the City of London continuing to be the global financial hub of the world in the long term.

The other indicator to examine is the current account as a percentage of GDP. Figure 5.12 includes this percentage alongside the actual current account balance. Until recently this proportion was fairly modest, generally fluctuating between 1% and 3% of GDP and below that of the late 1980s boom, when the deficit reached as high as 5% of GDP. As long as the country is generating sufficient income to be able to pay back the accumulating debt, then the current account deficit should not pose a problem. Economists believe that only when the deficit increases beyond about 5% of GDP that the government should have cause for concern. The US current account deficit is around 7% of GDP, for example. The chart indicates that recently the deficit was 4-4.5% of GDP at worst. Time is also a crucial factor: it is hoped that the UK will not run a large current account deficit indefinitely, but at the moment it appears to be within manageable limits.

Nonetheless, the record trade in goods deficit does indicate significant *structural changes and weaknesses in the UK economy*, especially the decline in manufacturing industry in the UK. It reflects the fact that UK goods are often of poor quality and design and poorly marketed, which is largely down to low investment levels and the UK productivity gap. It is also a sign that UK growth in recent years is rather *unbalanced, too heavily reliant on consumption, which is sucking in imports and not enough on investment and exports*, as was noted back in Chapter 1. Whether the collapse in consumer spending in 2008 and 2009 indicates that, the long awaited rebalancing of UK growth now underway remains to be seen. The trade in goods deficit is a significant problem for the UK given that it is a relatively open economy, with a high percentage of GDP accounted for by imports and exports.

Essay Question

6. (a) Explain the causes of the UK current account deficit. *(40)*
   (b) To what extent is the UK's current account deficit a cause for concern? *(60)*

● Analysis: The changing value of the pound

The value of the exchange rate compared to the currencies of the UK's major competitors is shown in Figure 5.13. The exchange rate is in a **free floating system**, which means that the Bank of England does not intervene to alter the value of the pound on the foreign exchange markets. The pound is therefore allowed to find its market or equilibrium rate. The pound rose rapidly between 1996 and 2001, and then remained broadly constant until 2006, when it rose again. Explanations for why the pound rose over these periods include:

- **Confidence** in the pound: the UK economy experienced continuous growth between 1992 and 2008. Speculators were confident that the economy was strong and they had confidence in the government's macroeconomic framework. Even during the global slowdown of 2001-2, UK growth remained relatively impressive.

- Higher interest rates: until 2008 the Bank of England's base rate was continually higher than the

Figure 5.13: The sterling effective exchange rate index (Jan 2005 = 100)

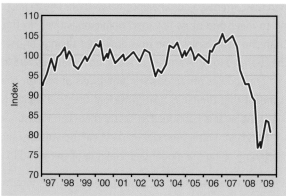

Source: Bank of England

European Central Bank rate and the Bank of Japan rate over the period shown, and at times it was also higher than the US rate. This may have led to an inflow of **hot money**.

• Inflows of FDI have been strong in the UK, especially in the financial services industry, concentrated in the City of London. The demand for pounds rose as a result.

• The strength of the pound was partly due to the weakness of the dollar, which in turn was partly down to the large US trade deficit.

The *consequences* of a strong pound include:

• Low inflation: the Bank of England's job was made easier by the high value of the pound, keeping imported inflation low, and reducing the need for higher interest rates.

• A worsening in price competitiveness of exports.

• An increase in import penetration: the strong pound means that Japanese TVs and clothes made in China that are purchased in shops such as Primark and Topshop have been very low-priced.

• Potentially, a reduction in aggregate demand and economic growth, as the value of imports has constantly exceeded the value of exports.

• A reduction in the profitability of UK companies based overseas: the weakness of the dollar has led to lower profits made by UK companies based in the US.

Figure 5.13 shows the dramatic fall in the value of the pound throughout 2007 and its collapse until the beginning of 2009. Reasons include:

• A collapse in confidence in the UK government's ability to manage the economy, as well as an expectation by the markets that the UK could be hit harder during the global slowdown than many of its competitors.

• Expectations of cuts in interest rates by the Bank of England during 2008, followed by the actual cuts themselves, from 5% in September 2008 to 0.5% by February 2009. This inevitably meant a reduction in hot money flows to the UK.

• But apart from these two factors it can be argued that the pound was overvalued relative to the dollar in the early 2000s and a downward correction was inevitable sooner or later. The strong pound made US and European goods very cheap, raising their demand and UK ones more expensive, reducing demand. Thus part of the fall in the pound after 2007 is a decline to a more 'realistic' level against both the dollar and the euro.

Question

7. Examine the consequences for the UK economy of a fall in the value of the pound.

Chapter 6
Productivity and Competitiveness

This Chapter examines recent trends in productivity in the UK compared with other industrialised countries before looking at measures of competitiveness which help account for these trends. Reforms which could raise the level of productivity in the UK economy and its position in the Global Competitiveness League are then considered.

● Knowledge: The meaning and relevance of productivity

Productivity measures the output produced by the economy relative to a given input, or set of inputs. The most widely used measure of productivity is **labour productivity**, or output per worker. However, given the fact that over time there are changes in the structure of employment, for example between full and part-time work, or in the number of hours worked for some other reason, such as working on Sundays or number of holidays, then output per hour worked is actually the more useful measure.

International competitiveness involves two aspects: **price competitiveness** and **non-price competitiveness**. Price competitiveness is determined by the economy's inflation rate, exchange rate and **unit labour costs**. Unit labour costs are calculated by dividing the average wage rate by the average product, or productivity. Price competitiveness can be calculated by taking the real exchange rate, which is the price of domestic goods relative to the price of foreign goods multiplied by the nominal exchange rate.

The importance of productivity growth:

(i)   It is arguably the most important indicator of living standards in the economy. Nobel prize-winning economist Paul Krugman states that "Productivity isn't everything, but in the long run it is almost everything."[1] If the productivity of resources is increased then an economy can generate more income or output per worker, increasing the standard of living and helping to eradicate poverty. Higher productivity growth will increase the economy's trend rate of growth, allowing real GDP to grow more quickly without the threat of inflation. However, because of the difficulties of calculating the productivity of certain types of capital, such as human capital, productivity tends not to be used as a measure of the standard of living, so real GDP per capita, the Human Development Index, or the ISEW (see Chapter 4), tend to be used instead. Nonetheless, there is no denying the importance of productivity growth in determining living standards.

(ii) Productivity growth keeps inflation low. If workers in the workplace operate more efficiently, then businesses are able to produce more goods and services at a lower average cost, or higher average product (productivity). If businesses are able to pass these lower costs on to the consumer and lower prices, then this will reduce cost-push inflationary pressure in the economy.

(iii) Productivity growth drives down **unit labour costs**, which will improve the international competitiveness of UK goods and services on world markets.

---

1. P. Krugman, *The Age of Diminished Expectations* (1999), 3rd edition.

The UK compares less favourably than France in terms of GDP per hour worked, as they work less hours than us.

● Application: Britain's relative productivity performance

Figure 6.1: International comparison of GDP per worker, 2007

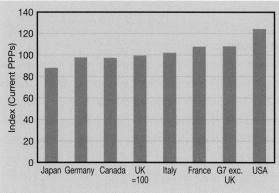

Source: ONS

Figure 6.2: International comparison of GDP per hour worked, 2007

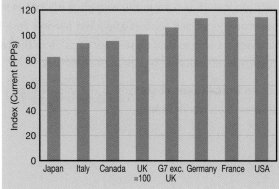

Source: ONS

Low productivity levels and growth rates are often cited as reasons for the UK's relatively low long term growth rate. Until recently, it was thought that the UK had a substantial productivity gap compared to its major competitors. This led to *The Economist* dubbing UK productivity "the missing guest at Gordon's party".[2] Interestingly, however, the latest data indicates that the productivity gap is less than when studies of the gap first began. Nonetheless, the UK still lags behind the rest of the G7 nations by an average of 8% as shown in Figure 6.1. This figure underlines the stark fact that the gap is still too large. Productivity figures are also given in terms of output *per hour worked* to take account of hours worked across countries. Figure 6.2 shows this productivity comparison. The UK performs more favourably on GDP per hour worked compared to countries that work longer hours, such as Japan, but less favourably compared to those who work fewer hours, such as France.

2. *The Economist*, 24 January 2004, p. 28.

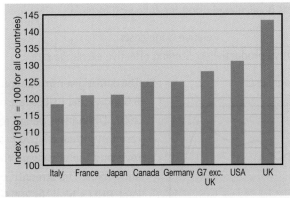

Figure 6.3: Productivity growth in the G7, 1991-2007

Source: ONS

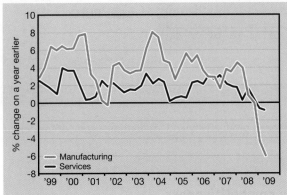

Figure 6.4: Growth in output per hour worked in UK

Source: ONS

Not only is the base level of labour productivity important, but so too, of course, is the *growth rate* of productivity over time. Figure 6.3 shows that since 1991 UK productivity growth of output per hour has outperformed all of the other G7 countries. The productivity of both manufacturing and services in the UK improved between 1999 and 2008. This is shown in Figure 6.4 which also indicates the collapse in productivity growth during the 2008-09 recession. This is because output declined during the recession, but the labour market tends to lag behind the business cycle. Businesses delay adjusting their labour force because of uncertainty over the length of the downturn.

The study by O'Mahoney and de Boer in 2002 indicated that there was a productivity gap in both sectors compared with the rest of the G7 countries.[3]

Question

1. Examine the consequences of the productivity gap for the UK economy.

● Application: Measures of competitiveness:

Figure 6.5: The sterling effective exchange rate index (Jan 2005 = 100)

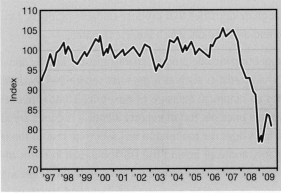

Source: Bank of England

Figure 6.5 shows the **sterling effective exchange rate**, which is a weighted index measuring the value of sterling against a basket of the currencies of the UK's major competitors. It indicates a slow worsening of price competitiveness from 1997-2007, although inflation remained relatively low and stable. The marked fall in the value of the pound from 2007-9 referred to above has improved price competitiveness and may allow UK companies to export more to help bring the economy out of recession.

3. 'Britain's Relative Productivity Performance', (2002), www.niesr.ac.uk.

We can compare unit labour costs between the UK and other countries by using a measure known as **relative unit labour costs**. This is calculated using the following formula:

$$\text{RULCs} = \frac{\text{Relative wage costs}}{\text{Relative productivity} \times \text{Sterling effective exchange rate}}$$

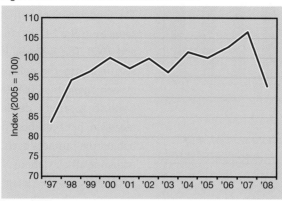

Figure 6.6: UK relative unit labour costs

Source: OECD

The data is given in index number form. Figure 6.6 shows that RULCs rose between 1997 and 2007. During this period relative wage rates rose faster than relative productivity growth, reversing the downward trend of the 1980s and 1990s. The strength of the pound also kept RULCs high. In 2007-8, the fall in the value of the pound, declining growth in wages and faster productivity growth combined to reduce RULCs.

Question

2. Explain the relationship between productivity and international competitiveness.

Extension material: Non-price competitiveness

Prices and costs are not the only determinant of competitiveness. Non-price aspects are also important. Non-price competitiveness can be measured in a number of ways. One way is to calculate the **income elasticity of demand** (YED) for UK exports and imports. The YED for imports is reckoned to be between 1.6 and 2, not significantly different to that of our major competitors, while the YED for exports is lower at between 1.0 and 1.5, which is lower than that of our competitors. This means that when world incomes rise UK imports will grow quicker than exports; this is especially true of the manufacturing sector. The reasons for this are:

• During an upswing firms tend to focus on the domestic market.

• UK businesses have insufficient productive capacity to satisfy both domestic and foreign markets.

• Investment has not grown enough in industries that produce tradable products: rather, investment has occurred in banking, insurance and distribution, which are less tradable.

Other measures of non-price competition include product characteristics, such as *quality*, *design* and *new product development*, and sales characteristics such as *after-sales service* and *marketing*. Calculating the value per ton of exports provides an empirical measure of non-price competitiveness as international competition should make the average price per ton of exports identical if goods are identical in terms of product and sales characteristics. UK values per ton tend to be lower than that of the US and Europe, and the UK lags behind the EU average, and well behind the US and Japan in terms of the proportion of manufactured exports in the 'up market' unit value category. However, the widespread embodiment in the UK since the 1980s of the Japanese approach to management, including initiatives such as TQM (Total Quality Management), has helped the UK improve in these areas in recent years.

● Analysis: Why is the productivity gap persisting?

Not only has the productivity gap been around for many years but also the **causes** of relatively poor productivity and competitiveness are the same as they have been for a number of years:

(i) A low percentage of GDP devoted to fixed capital investment spending

A rise in investment increases the capital stock available for each employed worker, which should boost labour productivity.

Figure 6.7: Investment as a share of GDP, 1994-2006, current prices

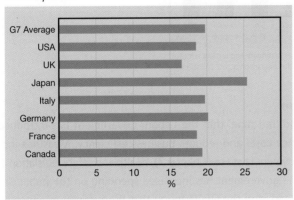

Source: Department for Business, Innovation and Skills

Figure 6.8: ICT spending as a % of GDP in 2004

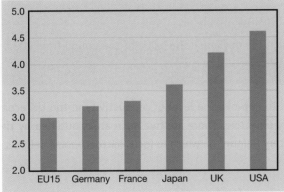

Source: HM Treasury

Figure 6.7 provides clear evidence of the fact that the UK has devoted a lower share of GDP to fixed capital investment spending than that of its major competitors. UK workers have a lower capital stock per head than that of the US, France and Japan. This has been an ongoing problem in the UK economy and relates to the short-termism that dominates the thinking of many UK businesses.

However, the UK has become more capital intensive since 1979, and its capital intensity has been rising by more than the US, France and Germany in recent years according to the study by O'Mahoney and de Boer in 2002. The IMF has recently defended the UK by arguing that the *quality* of investment spending is more important than the *quantity*. The IMF claims that UK investment in equipment is comparable to that of most OECD countries. However, the UK does fall short in the area of non-residential construc-tion investment, however. Since 1995, the UK has increased its rate of ICT capital spending growth significantly, and has started to close the gap on the US. Although it still lags behind the US, Germany and France, the

O'Mahoney and de Boer study suggested that the UK lies much closer to the latter two on this measure. Recent evidence from the Treasury suggests that the UK lies second only to the US as far as spending on ICT is concerned as shown in Figure 6.8. While government investment has started to rise as a percentage of GDP, it is still below most of our major competitors.

(ii) Lack of investment in human capital

The OECD suggested in 2004 that the UK compared poorly relative to its competitors on both basic literacy and vocational qualifications. Nearly a quarter of the adult population lacks basic literacy skills, more than double that of Germany, while a third of 25-34-year-olds have few or no formal qualifications beyond compulsory education. While the UK compares favourably on workers with high-level qualifications, it also has a higher percentage of workers holding the lowest level of attainment as is apparent in Figure 6.9. Too many people leave education early and relatively few get an apprenticeship, skilled craft or technician qualification, according to the OECD. This is another long-standing structural weakness of the UK economy that has kept productivity levels lower than its competitors for many years. This is surely the justification behind Tony Blair's 1997 election campaign that placed 'Education, education, education' at the forefront of the political agenda.

Figure 6.9: Distribution of 25-64 year old population, by highest level of education attained

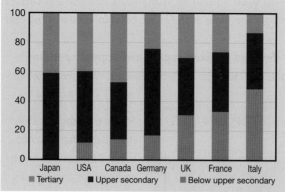

Source: OECD Education at a Glance. Upper secondary and tertiary refer to standardised levels of qualifications, to enable comparison across countries.

(iii) The burden of regulation

The number of regulations and 'red tape' that the Labour government has introduced since 1997 on businesses, increases compliance costs and reduces business efficiency. Measures include the national minimum wage and other employment laws (see Chapter 7), health and safety legislation and environmental legislation. Moreover, while the government has increased spending on the public sector significantly, productivity has failed to respond, and the OECD found that productivity in education and the health service has failed to improve beyond the growth rate of the early 1990s.

Question

3. Evaluate the extent to which the decline in the value of the pound from 2007-9 could help to improve UK competitiveness.

The government is determined to improve the level of productivity in the UK economy; indeed, the Treasury has cited this as a key objective. There are five main areas outlined by the Department for Business, Enterprise and Regulatory Reform[4] on which to focus microeconomic reforms, where the UK has struggled in the past:

(i) Investment

The need to encourage investment to improve the stock of physical capital in every sector and industry. Investment is still relatively low compared to our competitors and has reduced further during the 2008-9 recession. Government investment has increased in recent years, but still lags behind the US and France, while UK investment in infrastructure has been good recently. Inward FDI has been an important contributor to UK investment (see Chapter 3).

(ii) Innovation

The need to harness the potential of new ideas, technologies and working practices. Although the UK has a high quality science and engineering base, and scores highly on new and improved product development, it has a low percentage of GDP devoted to R&D spending as is shown in Figure 6.10 and we lag behind Japan, the US and Germany on patents per head. The UK does, however, have an innovative financial services industry and a big 'creative' sector, such as advertising, publishing, broadcasting and design.[5]

---

4. The 2008 Productivity and Competitiveness Indicators, www.berr.gov.uk.
5. 'Innovation and the Economy: The good, the bad and the ugly', *The Economist*, 4 August 2007.

*Figure 6.10: Gross domestic expenditure
on R&D as % GDP, 2006*

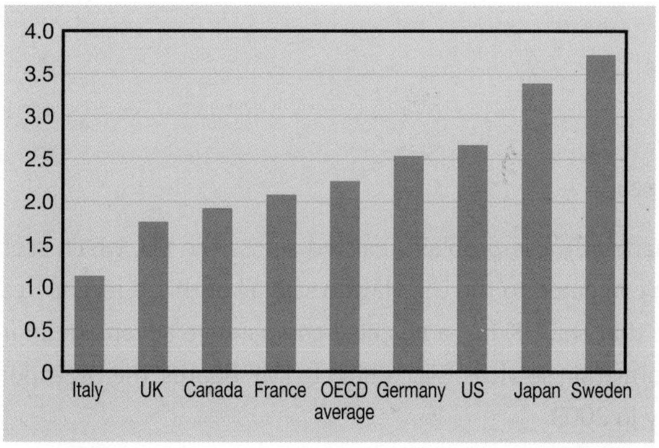

Source: OECD

(iii) Skills

The need to increase both the quantity and quality of skilled labour. The UK has a high proportion of people with degrees, but a low proportion of people with intermediate skills, leaving us with a high proportion of workers who have only low skills. The evidence also points towards a weakness in UK management performance.

(iv) Enterprise

The need for new and existing firms to take new business opportunities. It is relatively cheap to set up a business in the UK, though the UK does not have the culture of entrepreneurship as in the US. Access to finance is good, and efforts are being made to reduce the regulatory burden, which remains too high.

(v) Competition

The need to strengthen competition to encourage firms to innovate, reduce costs and improve the quality of goods and services. The UK scores highly on Competition Indicators, due to the highly-regarded Competition Policy (see Chapter 3), light product market regulation and openness to foreign competition.

A study by Porter and Ketels in 2003 had previously highlighted many of the strengths and weaknesses mentioned above, as well as policies that the UK can adopt in order to improve its international competitiveness.[6] These authors saw the following strengths:

- The deregulation, privatisation and labour market reforms of the Conservative government in the 1980s.

- The improvement in the macroeconomic framework with the switch to inflation targeting in the 1990s.

- The reform of competition policy in 2000 and 2002.

- The increase in asset building in the UK economy since the 1980s, including major investments in the transport infrastructure, education and the UK science base.

- Openness to international trade and investment.

- The relatively low level of regulation or 'red tape' required to set up a new enterprise.

- Low regulatory barriers to competition.

- The sophistication of UK capital markets.

---

6. M.E. Porter & C.M Ketels, *UK Competitiveness: moving to the next stage*, DTI Economics Paper No. 3.

But Porter and Kettels underlined several weaknesses, hampering UK productivity performance:

- A low skills base.

- Weak transport infrastructure.

- Low levels of R&D.

- A lack of access to debt finance.

The authors concluded that many of these problems existed across the EU, which scores relatively lower on many of these criteria when compared to the US. Having said all of this, a recent Treasury report on UK productivity provides evidence that the UK has a revealed comparative advantage in insurance, financial services, and computer and information services.[7] According to IMF figures, the UK exported more financial services than any other country in 2003.

Table 6.1: World Economic Forum Global Competitiveness League 2008-9

1	US	(1)
2	Switzerland	(2)
3	Denmark	(3)
4	Sweden	(4)
5	Singapore	(7)
6	Finland	(6)
7	Germany	(5)
8	Netherlands	10)
9	Japan	(8)
12	United Kingdom	(9)

Source: World Economic Forum (Last year's ranking in brackets)

Recent research by the World Economic Forum (WEF) provides a summary of these issues. The WEF's recent ranking of the competitiveness of global economies as shown in Table 6.1 puts the UK in twelfth place in 2008. The WEF praised the UK for the efficiency of financial markets and productivity gains as a result of technological advancements. However, the UK was criticised for its current macroeconomic environment, due to low saving, and a rising budget deficit and public sector net debt.

● Analysis: Policies to improve UK competitiveness

(i) Measures to boost UK fixed capital investment, such as the reduction in the rate of corporation tax

The government reduced the headline corporation tax rate from 30% to 28% in the 2007 Budget, although it increased the tax rate for small companies from 19% to 22%. Reducing corporation tax increases **retained profits** that firms can plough back into investment projects. This should help to boost the UK capital stock. It should also help the UK to keep attracting foreign direct investment.

(ii) Improvements in education, particularly vocational, in order to increase the level of intermediate skills

The government admits that there are still too many people in the UK with low literacy and numeracy skills. The government is increasing the share of GDP spent on education and ensuring that there is enough technical and vocational training such as apprenticeships. These measures should help to boost the level of **human capital**, a key determinant of economic growth.

(iii) Measures to encourage research and development

The government already provides R&D tax credits to encourage innovation for SMEs and large firms– the R&D tax credit for large companies was introduced in 2002. However, we have seen that the UK lags behind many of its competitors on R&D spending.

---

7. 'Productivity in the UK (6): Progress and new evidence', www.hm-treasury.gov.uk.

(iv) Reforms to reduce the regulatory burden on businesses

Since 2005, the government has appeared to acknowledge that UK businesses are over-regulated. Regulation needs to be high enough to protect UK employees whilst at the same time low enough to keep costs down and retain competitiveness

(v) Increasing government investment in infrastructure

Infrastructure includes roads, school, hospitals and public science. Government investment lags behind the UK's major competitors, and there is room for development in this area.

Question

4. Which of the following best represents a supply-side policy?
   A. A reduction in corporation tax to encourage more investment.
   B. Selling foreign currency to reduce inflation.
   C. Reducing the Bank of England base rate to reduce inflation.
   D. An increase in government expenditure on transfer payments.

● Evaluation: Are policies concerning productivity working?

Overall, the government has got some things right in terms of providing an environment conducive to higher productivity growth and competitiveness. The recent improvement in productivity is most welcome. The government has helped to provide macroeconomic stability, introduced a tougher competition framework, and provided an environment generally conducive to enterprise. The UK has a world-class university base, spending on education has increased and some progress has been made in improving skills. The cut in the headline rate of corporation tax is also welcome. However, the UK still lags behind its competitors in terms of fixed capital investment, R&D spending, intermediate skills, and the double whammy of the rising tax and regulatory burden is not conducive to further rising productivity and competitiveness.

Questions

5. Evaluate the effectiveness of the use of supply side policies to increase the level of UK productivity.

6. Examine the consequences to the UK economy of a lack of international competitiveness.

Chapter 7

Unemployment, Employment and Inactivity

In this Chapter we define the meaning of unemployment and compare the two measurements of the number out of work in the UK. We then note the differences in the data and trends shown by these two measurements before examining the reasons why UK unemployment fell between 1993 and 2004 and then those factors which explain why unemployment has since risen again. The Chapter discusses the changing state of employment levels and labour force inactivity. The Chapter ends comparing unemployment over the past two decades with the rate of price inflation.

● Knowledge: Defining unemployment

(i) **Unemployment** is defined as all those who are willing, available and able to work at the going wage rate in any suitable job but who cannot find employment.

(ii) The **unemployment rate** is the percentage of the economically active who are unemployed.

(iii) The **economically active** is all of those of working age (16 and over) who are either employed or unemployed.

(iv) The **economically inactive** is those of working age, but neither employed nor unemployed. It includes six categories of person:
   - Those in full time education.
   - Those who have taken early retirement.
   - Those who have given up searching for work.
   - Those who want to work but are not seeking work.
   - Those who have not actively sought work in the previous 4 weeks or are available to start within the next 2 weeks.
   - Those who are too ill or infirm to work. These people can claim Employment and Support Allowance (ESA, formerly Incapacity Benefit).

From 1945-76, the main macroeconomic objective of the UK government was to achieve full employment. Full **employment** is the highest possible employment at any given time, where all those who are willing and able to work are in employment, apart from those in **frictional unemployment**: workers in between jobs. Since the late 1970s emphasis has switched away from full employment towards price stability as the *main* macroeconomic objective. Full employment is nevertheless one of the current Labour government's four key macroeconomic objectives.

● Application: Measuring unemployment

Unemployment in the UK economy is measured in two ways:

(i) The **claimant count**: this is the number of people out of work and claiming Jobseekers' Allowance (JSA). The main problem with this measure is that it *excludes those who are seeking work but who may not be claiming benefit,* either because they are ineligible, or because they choose not to. Examples include:

(a) Those that have too high a level of savings.

(b) Those who have not built up enough national insurance contributions.

(c) Those that have a partner who earns a relatively high income.

(d) Those who feel embarrassed to claim benefit and therefore refuse to do so.

(e) Those that have left their job voluntarily.

(f) Those who have been dismissed for misconduct.

As a result the claimant count *understates* the true level of unemployment in the UK. On the other hand there may be a slight upward bias in the claimant count due to some people claiming benefit fraudulently!

(ii) The Labour Force Survey (LFS) measure as defined by the International Labour Organisation (the ILO): this is the *official* and the government's preferred measure of unemployment. It is a sample survey of around 61,000 households and 120,000 individuals carried out every three months. To be unemployed, individuals have to be *out of work, actively seeking work, have looked for work in the previous four weeks and be able to start work within a fortnight*.

Differences between the Claimant Count and the LFS figures

There are a number of reasons why the two measurements differ in both the levels and trends of numbers out of work:

(i) The LFS is regarded as more accurate than the claimant count; however, it still excludes part time workers and those who are not actively seeking work, but who would take a job if offered.

(ii) The LFS is used internationally, so comparisons between countries can be made (see Figure 7.8).

(iii) The LFS allows for more consistent comparisons over time than the claimant count, which was redefined many times during the 1980s and 1990s.

Figure 7.1: UK unemployment 1992-2009

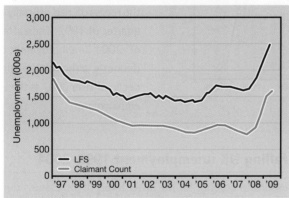

Source: ONS. All persons aged 16 and over, seasonally adjusted.

Figure 7.2: UK unemployment rates

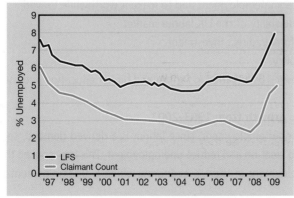

Source: ONS. All persons aged 16 and over, seasonally adjusted.

(iv) Since 1993, the claimant count has been well below the LFS as is evident in both Figures 7.1 and 7.2, but the two measures of unemployment were much closer during the recession of 1991-2. When employment is high and rising, more people will become ineligible for benefit since they are more likely to have too high a level of savings or they are more likely to have a partner earning too high an income. Also, individuals who have previously been inactive during a recession may be encouraged by the upturn in the economy and look for work. This means they become unemployed on the LFS, but they do not show up on the claimant count unless they begin claiming JSA. In a recession, some of those unemployed become *discouraged* and stop seeking work, so the LFS rises more slowly than the claimant count. In a recession it is more likely that the main earner in the family will be out of work, so their partner may become a job seeker and both will therefore qualify as unemployed on both measures.

Exam hint

At AS level you will be expected to be able to explain the different measures of unemployment and comment on the differences between these measures.

(v) In 2002, the LFS rose slightly but the claimant count continued to fall. At the time there was a lot of evidence to suggest that those who were being made redundant were refusing to claim benefit because of the social stigma attached. Many of the job losses were in middle management positions in the service sector and many of these individuals clearly did not want to 'lose face' by signing on. Therefore many people were out of work, but this did not show up in the claimant count figures.

Questions

1. Outline two differences between the claimant count and the Labour Force Survey measures of unemployment.

2. Explain why economists expected the gap between the claimant count and the LFS to narrow during the recession in 2009.

Figure 7.3: UK Real GDP growth and unemployment – a lagged relationship?

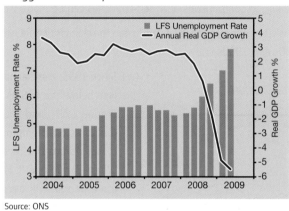

Source: ONS

Figure 7.1 shows how the unemployment level fell steadily in the UK after 1997 until 2004. Unemployment is a *lagging indicator*, which means that fluctuations in unemployment follow behind that of the economic cycle. The claimant count measure peaked in January 1993 at nearly 3 million, even though the recession had officially ended by the third quarter of 1992. Thereafter until the middle of 2004 unemployment fell almost continuously, although the speed of the descent declined after 2001 as the UK approached full employment.

● Analysis: Explanations of falling UK unemployment 1993-2004

We can identify at least seven reasons to account for the lower levels of joblessness during this period.

(i) Positive, stable economic growth from 1993-2007.

(ii) Active labour market policies such as the New Deal.

(iii) Measures to reduce voluntary unemployment and to make it worthwhile to work.

(iv) Measures to enhance the flexibility of the UK labour market.

(v) The substantial growth in foreign direct investment.

(vi) Reform of UK monetary policy.

(vii) The increased number of over-16s engaged in further and higher education and the falling birth rate.

(i) Positive, stable economic growth from 1993-2007

Economic growth stimulates higher employment, since labour is a derived demand, so a period of rising national output will increase job creation and reduce unemployment. This has reduced the level of **cyclical** or **demand-deficient** unemployment in the UK economy, which is unemployment that occurs when aggregate demand falls.

● **Evaluation of economic growth**

The UK's continued growth after 1993 is surely the dominant explanation of falling unemployment: it is no surprise that the biggest recent drops in the claimant count occurred in 1997 and 2000, the two years in which UK GDP growth was at its highest.

In contrast, unemployment often rises during a period of below trend economic growth, such as that experienced in 2001-2, as companies faced with declining profit margins attempt to control costs. However, the claimant count fell further over this period, while the LFS held stable. One reason for this may be Chancellor Gordon Brown's decision to increase spending on the public services between 2000 and 2006 (see Chapter 10), which led to significant job creation in the public sector. Another is the possibility that firms held onto their workforce because they expect demand to pick up in the future, meaning it would be costly to fire and then have to re-hire workers. This is known as **labour hoarding**.

(ii) Active labour market policies such as the New Deal

The government has taken measures to improve the employability of the UK workforce. The New Deal was introduced by the government in April 1998, which has helped improve the employability of the long term unemployed.

The New Deal aims to help young people find and keep a job, or become self employed. Jobseekers enter a 'Gateway' period in which they receive advice and guidance from the Employment Service. Each person is assigned a personal adviser who helps them build on the skills they have and learn new skills. Participants are given help with filling in application forms and producing an updated CV. Everyone between the age of 18 and pensionable age must go on the New Deal after a period of time in order to carry on getting benefit. This is six months for 18-24 year olds, eighteen months for those aged over 25. Sanctions such as withdrawal of entitlement to benefit are imposed on those who do not participate. Participants may go into full time education or training, the voluntary sector or join an Environmental Task Force if they cannot find a job or become self employed. The scheme was initially set up for young people between the ages of 18 and 24 but was subsequently extended to the long-term unemployed.

The New Deal aims to improve the skills of individuals and help them back into the job market. It should reduce **occupational immobility** in the labour market, reducing the amount of **frictional unemployment**, and making the labour market work more efficiently. The New Deal should also reduce **structural unemployment**, which occurs because of a long-term decline in demand for labour in traditional industries such as coal, steel and shipbuilding. The aim is to overcome the mismatch between the skills that employees possess and those required by employers in the 21st century labour market.

● **Evaluation of the New Deal**

The government believes that the New Deal is a crucial measure because it is specific to the needs of the individual worker and provides skills appropriate to the local community. It also claims that the scheme has significantly reduced long-term unemployment in the UK. Figure 7.4 shows that both the number of people out of work for more than a year and also those for more than two years declined significantly after 1998 until 2005. According to Pentecost and Sessions (2006), the New Deal has encompassed 2 million people, over 750,000 of whom have found jobs.[1] Blundell et al (2001) found that the introduction of the Gateway increased the probability by a third of the young long-term unemployed finding a job in the first four months of long-term unemployment.[2]

(continued overleaf)

---

1. E. Pentecost & J. Sessions, 'Labour Market Flexibility and Macroeconomics Policy in the European Union', in Vol. 22 *Development in Econ* EBEA, (2006).
2. R. Blundell, 'Evaluating the employment impact of the New Deal Gateway', IFS at www.ifs.org.uk.

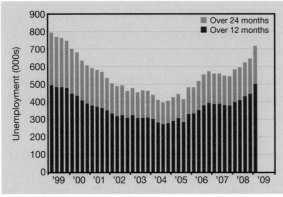

Figure 7.4: UK long term unemployment

Source: ONS

However, some groups of participants have been less successful than others. In particular, job entry rates for lone parents, 18-24 and 25+ had been "declining or stable for some years", according to a report by the House of Commons Public Accounts Committee in February 2008. Some of these workers may have found jobs anyway, and it is not clear exactly how long these workers held onto their jobs. In 2008 Channel 4 News reported an analysis from the London School of Economics which revealed that the New Deal raised the chance of people finding a job by between 5% and 7%. Evidence from the National Audit Office also suggests that only around 10% of successful participants kept their job for more than six months. The Channel 4 report concluded that those who found jobs exclusively because of the New Deal numbered less than 180,000. Some of the 750,000 mentioned in the 2006 study who have found jobs would have found jobs anyway even if it were not for the New Deal. This seems rather modest compared to a labour force of 30m, but still worth the money invested according to the LSE researchers. On balance, therefore, it would appear that the effect of the New Deal has been modest but positive. It has raised the skills base of some UK workers and helped to make the labour market work more efficiently. However, it is perhaps not the triumphant success that Gordon Brown has suggested!

(iii) Measures to reduce voluntary unemployment and to make it worthwhile to work

The government has sought to reduce the **replacement ratio** which is the ratio of out-of-work income to in-work-income, and also the **tax wedge** defined as the ratio of extra tax paid to benefits lost from working extra hours. This should minimise the effects of the **unemployment trap** (see Chapter 4). Policies introduced include:

(a) The introduction of the National Minimum Wage in 1999.[3]

(b) Cuts in the basic and starting rate of income tax.

(c) The introduction of the Working Families Tax Credit and Children's Tax Credit in 1999, subsequently replaced in 2003 by the Working Tax Credit and Child's Tax Credit.

(d) Reforms to the education system, including policies aimed at enhancing child and adult literacy and numeracy, should enhance skills levels and eventually close the UK productivity gap.

(iv) Measures to enhance the flexibility of the UK labour market

This has made it easier for employers to 'hire and fire' workers. The impact of this on the labour market was studied by the Treasury in 2003.[4] Flexibility has several dimensions:

(a) **Wage Flexibility.** This term means the reduction in trade union power and the tendency for wage bargaining to occur more at a local level have enhanced wage flexibility in the UK economy. The OECD believes that the UK has the most flexible real wages in the EU, with the exception of the Netherlands. There is also evidence that wages grow less rapidly in regions with higher unemployment in the UK. This all means that real wages should change quickly when demand and supply for labour change, reducing the length of time that the labour market is in disequilibrium. The recession of 2008-9 has shown that UK workers have been willing to accept a decline in wages and a reduction in working hours in return for keeping their jobs.

---

3. Be *very careful*, however, about using the minimum wage as a policy to reduce unemployment: neoclassical economists believe that a minimum wage, particularly a high one as the UK's now is, may lead to *real wage unemployment*. So far in the UK there is little evidence for this, however.
4. HM Treasury, *EMU and labour market flexibility* (2003).

(b) **Geographical mobility of labour.** This is fairly limited both within the UK economy and between the UK and members of the EU, despite free movement of labour in the Single European Market.

(c) **Temporal flexibility.** This term refers to the degree of flexibility in working time. The number of part-time employed in the UK has risen significantly in recent years, as has the percentage of total employment that is part time. The UK has a much higher proportion of part-time workers than most developed market economies, according to the OECD. However, a smaller percentage of workers are on temporary contracts than most of the rest of the EU.

(d) **Functional flexibility.** This concept refers to acquiring and using different skills. There is some evidence of skill shortages in the economy, especially concerning the level of intermediate skills. Though the UK compares favourably in terms of skilled workers, a high proportion also have low skills compared to Germany and other EU competitors. The Treasury, however, suggests that the lack of skilled workers is less of a constraint than it was back in 1997.

In the 2003 study the Treasury developed an overall index of labour market flexibility for the UK and its competitors. It included factors such as benefit duration, spending on New Deal, trade union coverage and so on. The study claimed that the UK had the second best flexibility score behind the US.

However, **labour market regulation** has undoubtedly increased under the Labour government. Examples include:

(a) The introduction, and subsequent increase beyond the growth of average earnings, in the National Minimum Wage.

(b) The 1999 Employment Relations Act, which promotes union recognition in the workplace.

(c) The implementation in 1998 of the EU Working Time Directive. This lays down regulations on matters such as how many breaks employees can take, holiday entitlements, and aims to limit the average working time for employees to 48 hours.

(d) The 2002 Employment Act, which lays down the entitlement to pay and time off for maternity and paternity leave, as well as ensuring minimum standards for disciplinary and grievance procedures.

This extra regulation may well have helped to improve industrial relations and led to a better balance between flexibility and social justice as well as helping to strengthen employment opportunities for women. However, the increased regulation has increased so called 'compliance costs' on UK businesses, and may have contributed to a lack of competitiveness. Small and medium-sized enterprises are hit especially hard by this regulation.

(v) The substantial growth in foreign direct investment (FDI)
Inward investment flows from multinational corporations were discussed earlier in Chapter 3.

(vi) Reform of UK monetary policy
The key new policy initiative of the new Labour government was to hand over the control of interest rates to the Bank of England through the Monetary Policy Committee (MPC). The work of the MPC has helped to reduce inflationary expectations, helping to curb wage demands, and reduce real wage unemployment. This is discussed in detail in Chapter 9.

(vii) The increased number of over-16s engaged in further and higher education, delaying their entry into the labour market
Coupled with the fall in the birth rate since the late 1960s, this has meant a reduction in the number of people of working age entering the labour market since the 1980s, and thus reduced the numbers that might not have found work and been unemployed.

● Analysis: Explanations of rising UK unemployment 2005-09

Figure 7.1 showed that the period of falling unemployment ended in 2005 and then the trend changed direction. How is this increase in joblessness explained?

(i) Slowdown and then recession

Real GDP growth fell below trend from the middle of 2004 to the end of 2005, and unemployment duly rose in 2005 and 2006. An acceleration in GDP growth in 2006 did reduce unemployment once again in 2007. However, the onset of slowdown and recession after 2007 led to a surge in cyclical unemployment in 2008 and 2009. By June 2009, the claimant count had risen to 1.56m, up from 788,000 in February 2008, while the LFS had risen to 2.47m, up from 1.58m in November 2007. The impact on jobs does not seem to have been industry specific: almost all sectors of the economy have been shedding labour. The highest profiles include financial services, retailers and construction companies.

(ii) A substantial rise in immigration

The effect of a growing number of immigrants is to increase the number of economically active. Remember the unemployment rate is the percentage of the economically active who are unemployed. So when the working population rises due to immigration and only some of these people may find jobs, then unemployment rises. The UK has thus experienced a rise in both employment and unemployment as a result of immigration.

(iii) An increase in the participation of older workers in the labour market

The number of people beyond normal retirement age looking for work has increased substantially due to better health in old age, inadequate pensions and more job opportunities.

(iv) A rise in the youth unemployment rate

There has been a marked rise in the number of young people out of work since 2005 as Figure 7.5 shows. This is due to:

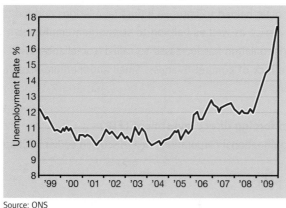

Figure 7.5: Youth unemployment, aged 18-24 years

Source: ONS

(a) Too many people leaving school without appropriate skills.

(b) The recession: the number of job vacancies declined significantly in 2008-9. Companies are even less likely to recruit younger workers who typically lack experience compared to older workers.

(c) The substantial increase in the national minimum wage rates for 18-21 year olds and 22+ between 2003 and 2006 may have priced younger workers out of the job market.

●● Analysis and Evaluation:
What has Labour done to try to stem the recent rise in UK unemployment?

The government have proposed several measures to attempt to curb the rise in the numbers out of work.

(i) Expansionary fiscal policy

The government plans to run a large budget deficit of 13% of GDP in 2009/10. This acts as an injection into the circular flow of income, creating a rise in aggregate demand and a multiplied rise in national income. This should prevent the demand for jobs from falling too significantly. However, vacancies have collapsed from 651,000 in June 2008 to 429,000 in June 2009. This represented both a record rate of decline and also a record low level of the number of vacancies. The government would argue, however, that vacancies may have declined even further had it not planned such a large budget deficit. Of course, there may be a negative impact on unemployment later when taxes rise in order to pay the debt accumulated as a result of the budget deficit.

(ii) Expansionary monetary policy

The Bank of England reduced interest rates from 5% in September 2008 to 0.5% by March 2009. The Bank has also undertaken quantitative easing (see Chapter 9): boosting the money supply. Together these policies have a similar effect on aggregate demand and national income as fiscal policy. If anything, monetary policy is more powerful as interest rates can be changed every month, whereas fiscal policy is often less flexible. However, there is a danger that this will fuel inflationary expectations and boost wage demands, increasing real wage unemployment. Of course it may be that at the moment individuals are happy simply to retain their jobs, or even work fewer hours, and wage demands may remain subdued. In addition, it was partly central banks keeping interest rates too low for too long that caused the recession in the first place, so it may seem odd that the cause of the problem is also the solution!

(iii) Wage subsidies

Since April 2009 employers can claim a subsidy of £1,000 if they recruit someone who has been unemployed for at least six months. From January 2010 any young person who has been out of work for more than a year will be guaranteed either employment or a place on a training scheme.

(iv) Support for job centres

The government has given more resources to Jobcentre Plus agencies in order to try to match up unemployed workers to those employers who do have vacancies. This should minimise the period of time taken in between losing a job and finding a new one, reducing **frictional unemployment**.

● Application: Regional unemployment

Figure 7.6: Regional unemployment, March-May 2009

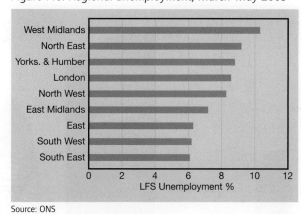

Source: ONS

The aggregate UK unemployment figures mask significant **regional disparities**, as is clear in Figure 7.6. In many parts of the South West and South East, such as Richmond-upon-Thames in London and Purbeck in Dorset, unemployment is below 4% on the LFS, and it could be argued that these areas are at, or are very close to, full employment. This has led to **skill shortages** in these more prosperous areas of the country. In contrast, unemployment in the West Midlands (10.3%), the North East (9.2%), and Yorkshire and the Humber (8.8%) is higher than that of the south east (6.1%), although the gap has narrowed significantly since the early 1990s. There are actually more significant disparities *within* regions than there are between regions: within London, unemployment in Richmond-upon-Thames (3.7%) is much lower than Tower Hamlets (11.3%), while within the North East and Cumbria, the unemployment rate in Eden is much lower than that of South Tyneside.[5]

---

5. Figures from March-May 2009 Labour Force Survey.

● Application: Unemployment – an international perspective

Table 7.1: The changing picture of unemployment in selected countries

	UK	France	Germany	Italy	Japan	US
1960-68	2.6	1.7	0.7	3.8	1.4	4.7
1983-97	9.5	10.5	6.2	7.9	2.7	6.4
2008	5.6	7.8	7.3	6.8	4.0	5.8

Source: Adapted from OECD (2002), www.oecd.org

Table 7.1 shows how the combination of economic growth, labour market policies, and demographic trends in the UK has improved the performance of the UK labour market in recent years. In the early 1990s, UK unemployment was above the G7 and OECD average. By 2003, UK unemployment had fallen to 5.0%, well below the 15 nations within the EU average of 7.8% and the OECD average of 7.1%. In 2009, UK unemployment was slightly higher at 7%, but still below the OECD average of 7.5%. It is true that the UK labour market is less regulated than that of the Euro area, but as the UK embraces EU legislation and as European countries gradually reform their labour markets to make them more flexible, the difference is becoming less marked. The UK has grown more rapidly than its competitors in recent years and this has helped keep UK unemployment well below that of some of its competitors. However, as Table 7.1 shows, unemployment is still well above that of the 'golden age' of the 1950s and 1960s. Moreover, Figure 7.7 demonstrates that some European countries such as the Netherlands and Norway are performing better than the UK on unemployment, as indeed is the United States.

Figure 7.7: Standardised ILO unemployment rates, selected countries, Q1 2009

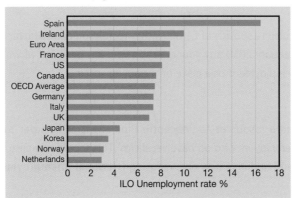

Source: ONS

Much job creation has come from financial services in the City of London.

● Knowledge: Employment levels

Employment and unemployment are not always the inverse of each other. This is because unemployment could fall if individuals gave up looking for work, but no jobs would have been created. In addition, if the working population is rising, then unemployment and employment could rise at the same time. If 20 Polish plumbers come to reside in the UK and seek work, and 10 of these plumbers get a job, then employment rises by 10. However, if the other 10 seeking work cannot find employment, then unemployment also rises by 10. In August 2005, for example, unemployment increased by 21,000 on the LFS, while employment also rose by 35,000.

● Application: Achieving an employment target

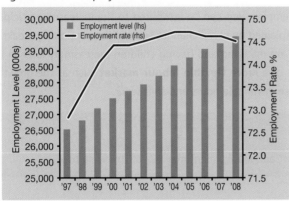

Figure 7.8: UK employment trends

Source: ONS. Employment level is all persons aged 16 and over.
Employment rate is % of population of working age in employment.

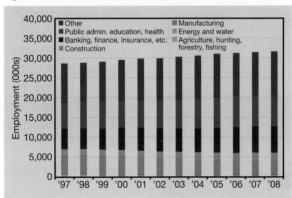

Figure 7.9: Growth in UK employment, selected industries

Source: ONS

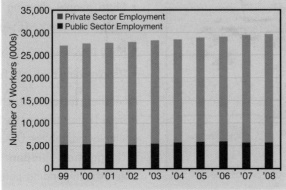

Figure 7.10 Distribution of UK employment by sector

Source: ONS

Employment in the UK fell during the recession of the early 1990s. After 1994, employment growth began to accelerate and in 2008 the level of employment peaked at over 29 million as shown in Figure 7.8. There was a net gain of nearly 4 million jobs in the UK between 1994 and 2008. Figure 7.8 also shows that the **employment rate** also rose between 1997 and 2001 because of economic recovery and growth, but it remained fairly stable up until the 2008-9 recession. Because the working population was growing, the employment rate did not quite get back to the previous peak level in 1990. The government's target is for the employment rate to rise to 80%. This looks somewhat unlikely over the medium term given that at the beginning of 2009, the employment rate collapsed at its fastest since records began in 1971, down to 72.9 per cent for the three months to May 2009.

The majority of job creation since 1996 has taken place in the service sector. Figure 7.9 illustrates how dominant a role the service sector now plays in the UK labour market. In 2008, 80.8% of all UK employment was in the service sector, compared to 74.9% in 1996 and 62.1% in 1979. Much of this job creation has come in the financial and public services, as the taller blue and red bars in Figure 7.10 indicate. There has been a huge level of investment by foreign banks and other financial companies in the City of London.

Construction has also been an area of growth since 1996, although given the small numbers involved this is less easy to tell from the graph. In contrast, there have been net job losses in agriculture, energy and water and manufacturing.

In a modern market economy it is inevitable that the pattern of demand will continue to shift away from the primary and secondary sector towards the tertiary sector. The strength of the pound sterling from 1996-2000 and again from 2004-7 also accounts for many of the job losses in manufacturing as was noted in Chapter 3. Manufacturing accounts for a large proportion of our exports, and much of our manufacturing output is exported. The 2008-9 recession hit manufacturing particularly hard and by June 2009 manufacturing employment was at a record low of 2.7 million, 1.8 million lower than in 1997. The performance of the service sector, in contrast, is much more dependent upon the state of the domestic economy, which we noted in Chapter 1 has remained buoyant over the last ten years.

The growth of public sector employment is down to massive investment in public services by Chancellor Gordon Brown, although note from Figure 7.10 that the growth of private sector employment has also been impressive, to the extent that the share of total employment accounted for by each sector has actually remained broadly constant over the last ten years.

Some of the recent growth in employment can be attributed to the increased participation of women in the labour force. This can be explained by social changes such as the continuing breakdown of traditional gender roles and that women are marrying and having children increasingly later in life. This has been facilitated by the development of a **more flexible labour market** such as the growth in part-time and temporary work and the increase in variable hours and shift work.

Question

3. Explain why unemployment and employment may rise at the same time.

● ● Application and Analysis: Inactivity

Figure 7.11: Number of economically inactive

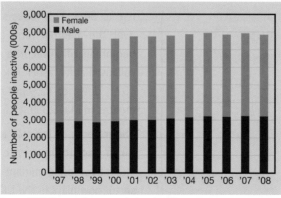

Source: ONS. Figures relate to population of working age.

Figure 7.12: Economic inactivity rates

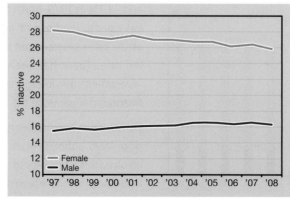

Source: ONS. Figures relate to population of working age.

There are now 7.9 million economically inactive people in the UK, compared with 6.7 million in 1990. Figure 7.11 makes it clear that the increase is almost entirely down to the growth in inactivity amongst men. The number of inactive males and the male inactivity rate have increased, while the female rate has steadily declined as shown in Figure 7.12.

The reasons for the growth of male inactivity are:

• The growth in the number of discouraged workers.

• More people claiming Employment and Support Allowance (ESA).

• More people taking early retirement.

• People going back into full time education.

All of these factors have led to claims that the official figures understate the 'true' level of unemployment in the UK, and that the UK is suffering from **hidden unemployment**. Given the impending pensions crisis, rising activity will be crucial in the future. In the

Figure 7.13: Number of economically active

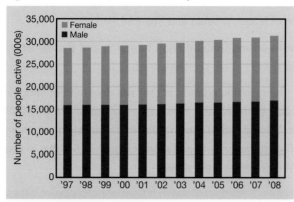

Source: ONS. All persons aged 16 and over.

Figure 7.14: Economic activity rates

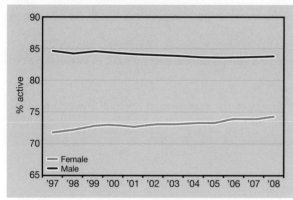

Source: ONS. Figures expressed as % of population of working age.

fourth quarter of 2006, 72% of males who were economically inactive did not want a job, while 36% were on long term incapacity benefit. Despite falling unemployment during the Blair years, the number of people on ESA in the UK was 2.6 million by the end of 2008, nearly double the level of 1990. People claiming ESA are expected to take appropriate steps towards finding work, more so than under the old incapacity benefit.

The number of economically active men and women has risen very gradually as Figure 7.13 shows but whereas the rate of activity for women has been rising slowly, the rate for men has been declining very slowly as Figure 7.14 shows. The continuing breakdown of the traditional gender roles means that the gap between the genders is narrowing slightly. It will not have pleased the Labour government that the number of economically active has only risen very slightly since 1997, as has the percentage of those of working age who are economically active.

● Analysis: The relationship between unemployment and inflation

Figure 7.15: Unemployment and inflation, 1988-2008

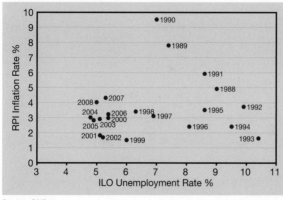

Source: ONS

Figure 7.15 displays the relationship between unemployment and inflation, for the UK economy in recent years. For the period 1988-1992, you could draw a classic Short Run Phillips Curve (SRPC) between the relevant data points. However, between 1993 and 2006, falling unemployment has failed to translate into higher wage inflation. The line of best fit along the data points for 1993-2006 is almost a horizontal line or, at least, a very flat SRPC! This may be due to the fact that the **Non-Accelerating Inflation Rate of Unemployment** (NAIRU) has fallen in recent years. The NAIRU is the rate of unemployment below which tightness in the labour market will lead to an increase in the rate of wage and price inflation. Economists have suggested the following factors have been instrumental in improving the unemployment/inflation trade off and reducing the NAIRU in the UK:

• Lower taxes and benefits and the introduction of tax credits.

• A fall in structural and long term unemployment.

• Higher labour productivity.

- Globalisation, increasing competitive pressures and reducing wage inflation.

- Privatisation and deregulation of labour, product and financial markets.

- Lower inflationary expectations arising from inflation targeting and the monetary framework of an independent Bank of England.

As far as policy is concerned, the recommendation is that the government should aim for a level of unemployment as close as possible to the NAIRU. However, estimates of the UK NAIRU vary wildly, and are subject to constant revision. This has led to some economists seriously questioning the usefulness of the NAIRU in a policy context. The alternative interpretation of Figure 7.15 is that of the Short Run Phillips Curve *shifting inwards*, for the reasons mentioned above.

Questions

4. Between November 2007 and June 2009 the rate of unemployment on the LFS measure in the UK rose from 1.58m to 2.47m. Examine the consequences of this for (i) unemployed individuals, (ii) the UK economy.

5. Evaluate the effectiveness of (i) a budget deficit, and (ii) a cut in interest rates to reduce the level of UK unemployment.

6. To what extent might the pursuit of full employment contradict with one other macroeconomic objective?

Chapter 8
Inflation and Deflation

This Chapter explains the different measurement of inflation by the Retail Price Index as compared with the newer Consumer Price Index and how they portray different trends in the general price level during the past decade. The Chapter looks at disaggregated price data before comparing inflation in the UK with that in other countries. Explanations for low price inflation until 2004 are offered before identifying reasons why inflation became more rapid thereafter. The Chapter ends with discussion of why a falling price level – deflation – is an unwelcome situation.

● ● Knowledge and Application: Defining and measuring UK inflation

Inflation is defined as a sustained increase in the general price level, or a fall in the purchasing power of money. Inflation occurs when the prices of *all goods and services together* are rising *on average*.

There are two main measures of inflation in the UK that you should be able to define and explain in an examination:

1. RPI – Retail Price Index
The RPI is a weighted index measuring the annual increase in price of a basket of 650 goods and services. Each product in the shopping basket is weighted according to the proportion of expenditure allocated by the average household on each category. The weights are taken from the Expenditure and Food Survey and are revised every year to take account of changes in households' expenditure patterns and technology. Every year the goods and services that make up the RPI are also changed. For example, in 2009, parmesan cheese replaced imported cheddar and MP4 players replaced MP3 players. Other new items for 2009 include DVD internet rental (e.g. Lovefilm) and Blu-Ray discs.

In the Expenditure and Food Survey, over 6000 households record their expenditure over a two week period. This data is then used to calculate the weights allocated to each group. For example, if on average households spend twice as much on housing and household services as they do on clothes, then housing and household services carries twice the weighting that clothes does.

2. The CPI – Consumer Price Index
In December 2003, Chancellor Gordon Brown announced a change in the inflation target to the *Harmonised Index of Consumer Prices* (HICP) measure, thereafter renamed the **Consumer Price Index** (CPI). The inflation target for the CPI was set at 2.0% per year. The reason for the change in the inflation target is to allow UK inflation to be compared with inflation in the EU. The HICP was developed initially to assess whether EU member states would meet the inflation convergence criterion for monetary union (see Chapter 11). It now acts as the measure of inflation monitored by the European Central Bank to assess price stability in the Eurozone.

Figure 8.1: RPI group weights 1987

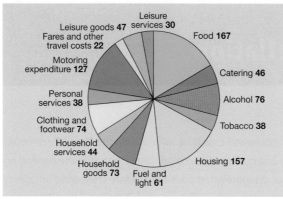

Source: ONS. Total = 1000.

Figure 8.2: RPI group weights 2009

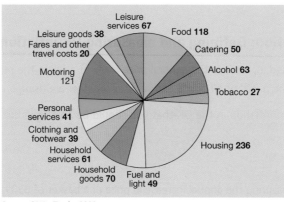

Source: ONS. Total = 1000.

Data Questions

1. Explain the possible reasons for the decline in the share of spending between 1987 and 2009 on (i) Food, from 167 to 118, and (ii) Clothing and Footwear, from 74 to 39.

2. Calculate the percentage increase in the share of spending allocated to (i) Housing, and (ii) Leisure Services between 1987 and 2009.

3. Explain the possible reasons for the increase in the shares of spending that you have calculated in response to Question 2.

Extension material: The continuing relevance of the RPI

Although the Bank of England is not set a target based on the RPI, the measure is still used by the government for uprating of pensions, benefits, and in indexing government securities, or gilts. It is often cited by trade unions as a benchmark for pay negotiations, and acts as a basis for indexing tax allowances. This means that the RPI is still an important and closely tracked measure, and it is still arguably the best representation of the change in the average cost of living in the UK economy.

Question

4. Which of the following best explains how the rate of inflation is measured?
   A. The level of the CPI (Consumer Price Index).
   B. Changes in the relative prices of goods and services.
   C. Taking the percentage change in prices that goods leave the factory gate.
   D. Calculating the percentage change in the price level between two time periods.
   E. Calculating the difference between the price level this year and the price level last year.

● Knowledge: Explaining differences between the RPI and CPI

There are some important differences in the way the two indices are constructed.

(i) The weights for the CPI are based on the expenditure of all private households in the UK, foreign visitors to the UK, and others such as residents of nursing homes. The weights are taken from the national accounts, not the Expenditure and Food Survey. In contrast, the RPI excludes the top 4% of income earners as well as pensioner households, as these groups have spending patterns that are very different from the general population.

(ii) The CPI excludes a number of housing costs which the RPI includes, such as council tax and rates, mortgage interest payments, housing depreciation and dwelling insurance and ground rent.

(iii) The RPI excludes university accommodation fees, foreign students' university tuition fees and unit trust and stockbroker charges, all of which are included in the CPI.

(iv) The RPI is calculated using an arithmetic mean while the CPI uses a geometric mean.[1]

●● Application and Analysis: Explaining the difference between trends in the RPI and CPI

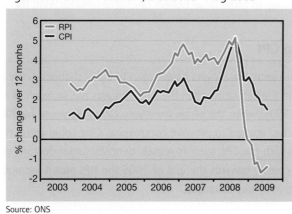

Figure 8.3: UK RPI and CPI, Dec 2003 - Aug 2009

Source: ONS

Figure 8.3 compares the movement of both measures of inflation since the CPI was introduced in December 2003. Until recently, the CPI was almost always lower than the RPI, because of:

(i) Differences in housing costs
The CPI excludes most components of owner occupied housing costs. The CPI tends to be lower than the RPI because these housing costs often rise more quickly than other prices.

(ii) The formula effect
Geometric means tend to give slightly lower figures than arithmetic means, and give less weight to items in the index whose price is rising more rapidly.

(iii) Differences in coverage of other goods and services and weights
The main reason for the difference in the two indices in December 2003, at the time the CPI first appeared, was due to 'other housing costs', i.e. housing depreciation and council tax (which we noted above are part of the RPI). The widening of the series' over the year 2004 reflected the fact that the Bank of England raised interest rates three times that year, which raised mortgage interest payments and raised the RPI in relation to the CPI. Thereafter, however, interest rates were stable at 4.75% for a year, and then a 0.25% cut saw interest rates stable at 4.5% for another year.

The decline in the rise in housing costs in 2005-6 meant that the RPI and CPI converged and became much closer. But in 2006-7, the RPI rose well above the CPI due to the five quarter point interest rate increases between August 2006 and June 2007. Three 0.25% interest rate cuts between December 2007 and September 2008, and a fall in housing depreciation added downward pressure to the RPI, meaning that the CPI was higher than the RPI in September 2008 for the first time in seven years (remember, mortgage payments and housing depreciation are not counted in the CPI). The steep drop in interest rates to 0.25% between September 2008 and May 2009 was the main reason for the RPI dropping much more rapidly than the CPI over that time.

---

1. For those readers who are into statistics, the arithmetic mean is $\Sigma x/n$, whereas the geometric mean is $((X1)\,(X2)\,(X3)\ldots(Xn))^{1/n}$.

● Evaluation: The RPI and CPI compared

According to the ONS, the main explanation for differences in the RPI and the CPI tends to be that the CPI excludes most housing costs. This factor is much more important than the formula effect and differences in weights, whilst other differences in coverage of goods and services is the least important.

We can make some other comments about the two indices:

(i) The RPI and CPI are *average* measures of inflation. In reality, different groups in society such as pensioners and students, and indeed different individuals, will have their own rates of inflation.

(ii) The RPI and CPI are poor at picking up changes in the *quality* of durable goods. If you are buying a car today, you get an awful lot more for your money than you would have 25 years ago, such as electric windows, air conditioning, air bags, and iPod jacks!

(iii) Price data is collected from a wide variety of retail outlets. However, the RPI may not account for the fact that consumers may switch to other retail outlets (and other products) in the short term.

Extension material: Using the CPI

Both the government and private sector employers have begun to index changes in the wages and salaries of their employees to changes in the CPI rather than the RPI. This was not so much of an issue at the end of 2004 and the beginning of 2005, when the series were very close. However, by 2007, the series had clearly diverged and the policy had started to provoke controversy. One could argue that those who had wages and salaries rising in line with the CPI, such as nurses, dentists, junior doctors, and some teachers, were taking a real pay cut! Of course, towards the end of 2008 the RPI nosedived and these individuals could then claim to be receiving 'real' pay increases!

● ● Application and Analysis: Recent trends in UK inflation

Figure 8.4: UK CPI and RPI, 1997-2008

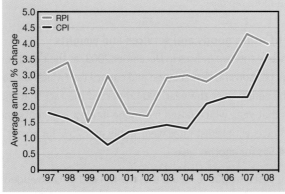

Source: ONS

Annual RPI inflation peaked at 9.5% in the year 1990 following the credit boom of the late 1980s. Between 1992 and 2004, however, UK inflation remained remarkably low and stable on all three measures. Figure 8.4 tracks the RPI and CPI between 1997 and 2009. In the 'mini boom' of 1997, the newly independent Bank of England increased interest rates from 6% in April of that year to 7.25% in November to try to choke off the threat of inflation. This duly succeeded and inflation fell steadily throughout 1998 and 1999. This allowed interest rates to fall back to 5% by June 1999. Inflation was then so low and stable that the economy enjoyed three long periods of stable interest rates: February 2000-February 2001, when base rates remained at 6%, November 2001-January 2003, when rates remained at 4%, and August 2004-July 2006, a remarkable period during which the base rate was changed only once.

However, the aggregate inflation figures can hide differing trends in inflation in goods and services. Several factors account for the different trends once we disaggregate the data.

(i) Figure 8.5 shows that between 1997 and 2006, inflation in goods either increased very slowly or, at times, such as between 2000 and 2004, it was actually negative: that is, the general price level of goods fell.

Figure 8.5: CPI in goods and services 1997-2009

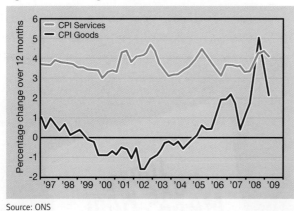

Source: ONS

Figure 8.6: Changes in consumer prices of selected goods and services, 1999-2008

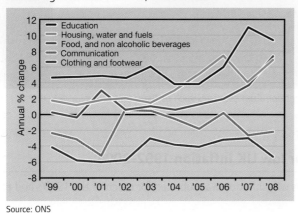

Source: ONS

(ii) In contrast service sector inflation has increased far more quickly, typically between 3% and 5% over the last 5 years.

(iii) Inflation in both goods and services gathered momentum since the middle of 2005, though price increases are most marked in services.

(iv) The sectors that saw the largest increases between 2005 and 2006 were housing and household expenditure and fares and other travel costs, while on the CPI, education saw a large increase thanks to large rises in private school fees and, in 2006, the introduction of variable top-up fees for degree courses.

(v) In 2007 and 2008, there was a significant increase in the price of food and fuel, which helped to boost the CPI to over 5% by the end of 2008.

(vi) In contrast, the price level of clothing and footwear and communication has been decreasing since 2003 as is apparent in Figure 8.6.

● Application: International comparison of inflation rates

Figure 8.7: Average annual change in CPI 1999-2008

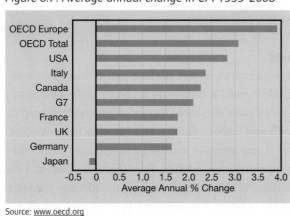

Source: www.oecd.org

Once dubbed 'the sick man of Europe' because of its poor inflation record, the UK's recent inflation performance compares more favourably with that of its major competitors. Figure 8.7 shows that on the CPI measure the UK has recently enjoyed low rates of inflation comparable with that of its major competitors, with the exception of Japan, which has experienced deflation. But it could be that the days of relatively low and stable inflation in the UK are coming to an end. In 2007-8, the UK CPI just nudged higher than the G7 average, and it is moving towards the OECD average as well, though it remains well below the OECD averages. Undoubtedly, however, the UK has performed better both in absolute and relative terms than was the case during the turbulent 1970s and 1980s.

The UK has faced increased competition from countries such as India and China.

● Analysis: Explanations for low UK inflation 1992-2004

We can identify several reasons why inflation was subdued for much of the 1990's and early in the present century.

1. Competitive product markets due to globalisation, privatisation and deregulation.
2. More flexible labour markets due to deregulation, migration, rising female participation.
3. Good fortune because of an absence of oil shocks, and the impact of a strong pound.
4. Active monetary policy.

We briefly consider each of these four explanations.

1. Competitive product markets

(i) Globalisation: as more and more countries have become part of free trade areas, competition at a regional level has increased, and forced UK businesses to reduce profit margins by reducing mark-ups on prices. Countries like the UK have also faced increased competition from newly industrialised countries such as China, India and Eastern Europe. This has effectively doubled the global labour supply. As these countries are labour intensive and have a *comparative advantage in labour-intensive products*, the UK has been importing more products from these countries at a cheaper price. Figure 8.6 revealed the big drop in clothing and footwear prices in the RPI over the last ten years as well as the deflationary effects in communication, due to cheaper telecommunication costs, and furniture and household goods, for example audiovisual items.

(ii) Privatisation and deregulation programmes in the 1980s and 1990s. These have helped to enhance competition in the utility sector, leading to downward inflationary pressure over the last fifteen years.

2. More flexible labour markets

(i) In the UK, the **deregulation of the labour market** in particular has reduced wage inflationary pressure. The deunionisation of the labour force has reduced the bargaining power of employees in many industries.

(ii) Inflow of migrant workers from the countries that acceded to the EU in 2004, such as Poland, increasing the labour supply in certain industries and reducing wage inflationary pressure.

(iii) Rising female participation in the labour force, which has helped to subdue wage inflation.

3. Good fortune

(i) The period of the 1990s was one characterised by a relative **absence of major inflationary shocks**, such as oil price shocks, compared to the 1970s and 1980s. There was a mild oil price shock in 1999, but thereafter in 2001 the oil price quickly fell again.

(ii) **Strength of the pound**: As noted in Chapter 5, a higher exchange rate reduces the price of imported raw materials, thereby reducing cost-push inflation. It also reduces the price of finished goods and therefore directly reduces the RPI. This is an especially significant factor for a relatively open economy such as the UK, which has a high degree of import penetration. We noted in Chapter 1 that imports account for 28% of UK GDP on the expenditure approach. Between 2000 and 2003 the pound fell relative to the euro, but thereafter it rose relative to the dollar and it remains relatively high compared to the early to mid-1990s, helping to control inflation.

4. Active monetary policy

Between 1997 and 2007 the Bank of England's Monetary Policy Committee was successful in setting interest rates so as to control inflation close to its target. The MPC raised interest rates *pre-emptively*, at the first sign of a positive output gap, to try to choke off inflation before it got going. *Inflationary expectations were reduced* due to the credibility of the Bank of England's monetary framework and the success of inflation targeting in the UK. This kept a lid on wages during the wage bargaining process.

● Analysis: Reasons for higher UK inflation 2004-08

Figure 8.5 showed that the first decade of the new century saw a revival of inflationary pressure. What accounts for this outcome?

(i) Higher oil prices

Oil prices tripled between 2004 and 2007, and by the middle of 2008 the price of Brent Crude was touching $140 a barrel, as shown in Figure 8.8, leading to cost push inflation in the UK economy. However, the oil price did *not* stay high enough to lead to 'second round effects', meaning that higher energy prices prompted trade unions to bid up their wage demands, resulting in a further round of higher prices and higher wages. Instead, the oil price fell back to just over $40 per barrel by the beginning of 2009. Moreover, the UK economy is a lot less dependent on oil than it was in the 1970s. Thus, rising oil prices today do not have the same inflationary effects as they did in 1973 and 1979. Nonetheless, oil prices still have a significant effect on gas and electricity bills and therefore on the costs faced by businesses and households.

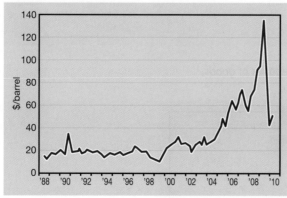

Figure 8.8: ICE Brent crude oil closing prices

Source: oilnergy.com

(ii) Higher food prices

Food prices rose by 12.2% between July 2007 and July 2008, though by May 2009 this pressure had eased somewhat.

(iii) The fall in the value of the pound

Figure 8.9: The sterling effective exchange rate index (January 2005 = 100)

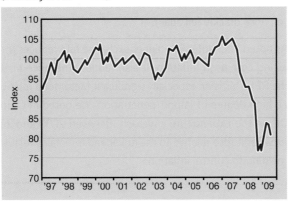

Source: ONS

Between the middle of 2007 and 2009 the sterling exchange rate fell. This causes upward pressure on the price of imported finished goods and raw materials, leading to imported inflation. Figure 8.9 shows the dramatic change in the sterling exchange rate in 2007.

Extension material: 'Core' inflation

The concept of core inflation is a measure of inflation that excludes volatile items like food prices and energy prices. It is thus a good guide to 'underlying' inflationary pressure in the UK economy. Core inflation did not rise dramatically in 2008 whereas the rise in the RPI and CPI was largely down to rising food and fuel prices. Core inflation may remain weak in 2009-10 due to the fall in aggregate demand.

Questions

5. Explain what is meant by the phrase 'sterling effective exchange rate index, January 2005=100' in Figure 8.9.

6. With reference to Figure 8.10, and your own knowledge, explain the possible reasons for the changes in the prices of the following items:
   (i) Food
   (ii) Fuel and light
   (iii) Clothing and footwear

Figure 8.10: RPI changes in categories of goods, July 2007-July 2008

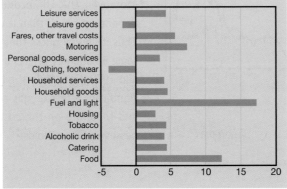

Source: ONS

Knowledge: Deflation

Deflation is the opposite of inflation and refers to a fall in the general price level in the economy. Although this may sound initially like a good thing, it is important to distinguish between 'good' deflation and 'bad' deflation.

(i) 'Good' deflation happens because of productivity improvements and technological advances which shift long run aggregate supply to the right, leading to economic growth without inflation.

(ii) 'Bad' deflation happens because of a fall in aggregate demand. It is this kind of deflation that has affected the Japanese economy since 1998 and that it is feared may affect the UK in the near future. As Figure 8.3 showed earlier, the RPI was already decreasing, i.e. the % change in the RPI was negative, in March 2009. The problem will come if there is a *sustained fall* in the general price level, i.e. if the level of the RPI and CPI continually fall.

Analysis: Reasons why deflation due to lack of AD is a problem

There are several concerns if an economy becomes subject to deflation:

(i) If consumers see prices falling today, they may believe that prices are going to fall tomorrow. They may therefore postpone their purchases until later, when they can get a better deal, reducing consumer spending. This leads to a fall in aggregate demand, which further reduces the general price level, setting off another round of postponed purchases and falling prices.

(ii) A fall in the general price level increases the real value of debt. This weakens the financial position of already indebted households, meaning they will take longer to pay back the debt. This leads to a reduction in consumer spending and a reduction in aggregate demand, which further reduces the general price level. This was first pointed out by noted economist Irving Fisher, and has become known as **Fisher's debt deflation**.

(iii) Deflation can reduce the power of monetary policy. If say, the Bank of England reduces interest rates by 2% in a year, but prices fall by 3% that year, then the **real interest rate** has increased by 1%. The only answer is for the Bank to reduce its rate further, but if deflation continues, the real rate will not decrease, unless the Bank cuts interest rates quickly enough. The problem here is that if interest rates were low to begin with, the Bank could end up with 0% interest rates very quickly! Monetary policy is impotent. This is what happened in Japan in the 1990s. By March 2009 the Bank of England's base rate was at 0.5% and the Bank decided that they had reduced rates as low as they could.

(iv) The impotence of monetary policy could lead to the government having no choice but to run a large deficit to kick-start aggregate demand. This could lead to a rapid rise in the national debt in the long run. Again, this is what happened in Japan, and with government debt forecast to rise to 80% of GDP, it looks like it could happen in the UK too.

Harder Questions

7. Using an AD/AS diagram, analyse the effect of a rise in the oil price on the UK economy (note: UK now net oil importer).

8. Evaluate the effects of a fall in the Bank of England base rate from 5.0% in September 2008 to 0.25% in March 2009 on the UK economy.

9. Examine how a rising rate of inflation may affect UK macroeconomic performance.

10. Evaluate the benefits for the UK economy of low inflation.

Chapter 9

Monetary Policy in the UK

Monetary policy is defined as the use of interest rates, the money supply and other policy instruments to control the amount of money and credit, and the terms and availability of credit in the economy. Until recently, monetary policy basically meant the use of interest rates to control aggregate demand. In 2009, however, the Bank of England tried to increase aggregate demand using a more unconventional method known as **quantitative easing**. The work and impact of the Monetary Policy Committee of the Bank of England is the focus of this Chapter. We consider the merits of inflation targeting and how changing interest rates can alter the level of economic activity. The Chapter ends with discussion of the recently-introduced policy of boosting the money supply through quantitative easing.

● ● Knowledge and Application: The UK monetary policy framework

In May 1997, the newly-elected Labour government surprisingly granted operational independence to the Bank of England. Under the 1988 Bank of England Act the Bank was given operational responsibility for setting interest rates in order to achieve the objective of **price stability**, and to support the government's economic policy, including its objectives for growth and employment. The Monetary Policy Committee (MPC) makes operational decisions on interest rates, comprising the Governor and Deputy Governor of the Bank, and seven other members, from academics to industrial and city economists.

The MPC's job is to set the base rate in order to hit the inflation target. The base rate is the Bank of England's interest rate: in simple terms, the rate at which it will lend to the money markets. It is also known as the repo rate. Since December 2003, the inflation target has been 2.0% per year on the CPI measure of inflation, with a margin of error of plus or minus 1% from the central point target of 2.0%. The target is *symmetrical*: which means that undershooting the target is supposed to be taken as seriously as overshooting.

The base rate is set by the MPC to ensure that the CPI will hit its target in exactly two years time because it takes time for interest rate decisions made today to feed into aggregate demand and inflation tomorrow. So the base rate is not changed every time the CPI deviates from its target. Rather, it is set at the level which the MPC believes will give the best chance of hitting the 2.0% target in two years time. In this sense the MPC is said to be *pre-emptive* in its decision making. This means that is forward looking, trying to anticipate or predict the need for a change in interest rates in order to reduce the volatility of inflation and interest rates.

Examples of 'pre emptive' decision making by the MPC include:

- 2001: the MPC cut interest rates no fewer than seven times to (successfully) choke off the threat of recession in the UK economy, despite inflation being below target at the time. (Figure 9.3 shows the movements of the base rate between 1999 and 2009.)

- July 2007: the MPC raised interest rates by a quarter of a percentage point to 5.75%, despite the fact that the CPI was falling back towards its target.

- October 2008-March 2009: base rates were cut drastically from 5% to 0.5%, despite inflation at the time being above target. This strategy was due to the onset of recession with the MPC believing that declining aggregate demand in 2008 and 2009 would lead to a reduction in 'core' inflationary pressures in 2009 and 2010.

On the first Wednesday and Thursday of every month, the MPC meets to decide whether or not to adjust the base rate. The committee considers a wealth of data, including consumer spending, investment, the government budget balance, the value of exports and imports, bank lending, wages, unemployment, productivity, oil prices, and developments in the international economy. When deciding whether or not to change interest rates, the MPC is trying to evaluate the strength of domestic demand relative to the economy's long term capacity to supply. If a positive output gap is forecast, it is likely that inflation will rise above its target in two years time, and the Committee will have to raise interest rates. If the output gap is forecast to be negative, rates will have to be reduced, and if there is no output gap, inflation is likely to hit the target and so interest rates are likely to be left on hold. One of the reasons for the Bank's decision to raise rates three times in 2007 was because domestic demand had been growing robustly and that UK businesses were close to reaching capacity constraints.

On the basis of this data the members of the MPC form a judgement on the likely course of inflation over the next two years. They must consider whether or not the CPI will hit the target of 2% in two years if no action is taken. If a majority of the committee believe that the CPI will hit the target then the committee leaves the base rate at the same level. If a majority believe that inflation is to miss its target then the MPC changes the base rate.

Questions

1. The Monetary Policy Committee (MPC) is most likely to decrease interest rates if:
   A. Unemployment is falling.
   B. The exchange rate is low and falling.
   C. The rate of growth of actual GDP is below the rate of growth of potential GDP.
   D. The rate of growth of the money supply is increasing.

2. Explain how the output gap would influence the Bank of England in setting interest rates.

UK monetary policy will only be successful if the policy framework and the central bank have established *credibility* amongst the public. In the UK, every effort has been made to achieve this.

(i) The MPC is comprised of members with a variety of backgrounds, including monetary policy experts, academics and economists from industry (see latest membership below).

The 9 members of the Monetary Policy Committee (as of October 2009)

Mervyn King	Governor of the Bank of England
Charles Bean	Deputy Governor responsible for monetary policy
Paul Tucker	Deputy Governor responsible for financial stability
Spencer Dale	Executive Director, Chief Economist
Paul Fisher	Executive Director, Markets, former Head of Foreign Exchange Division
Kate Barker	Former Chief Economist, CBI
Tim Besley	Kuwait Professor of Economics and Political Science, LSE
Andrew Sentance	former Chief Economist and Head of Environmental Affairs, BA
Adam Posen	Senior fellow at the Peterson Institute for International Economics (PIIE)

Source: Adapted from www.bankofengland.co.uk

(ii) The 1998 Bank of England Act has made monetary policy making more transparent and accountable. The minutes of every MPC meeting are published in the second week after the meeting, and can easily be downloaded from the Bank's website. The minutes also reveal how each member voted.

(iii) If the CPI strays more than 1% either side of the 2% target then the Governor of the Bank, Mervyn King, is obliged to write a letter to the Chancellor to explain why this occurred and what he will do about it. This happened on eight consecutive months between April and December 2008!

(iv) The MPC itself is accountable to the Court of the Bank, which comprises experts from industry, commerce and finance, and has to submit a monthly report on its actions. It is also accountable to Parliament, as the Treasury Committee has two sessions per year in which MPs can question MPC members and Bank officials on their actions.

(v) The Bank publishes its **Inflation Report** every quarter, in which it reviews developments in the economy generally, and monetary policy in particular, and explains and justifies its actions.

● Analysis: Why does the UK have an inflation target?

There is merit in requiring the MPC to have a 2% target.

(i) Experiments in the 1980s with targeting **intermediate variables**, such as various money supply measures and the exchange rate, failed. For example, in the 1980s when the government was trying to reduce the rate of growth of the money supply, money demand was unstable due to the deregulation of the financial system, which freed up banks' ability to lend money, for which there was no shortage of demand. Rather than targeting variables whose relationship with inflation is, at best, uncertain, the authorities should target inflation itself. It means that *all* available information relating to inflation can be used rather than getting side tracked by the performance of one variable.

(ii) It should reduce **inflationary expectations**. As long as workers believe that the target will be achieved, they will moderate their pay claims, which will reduce wage inflation. Similarly, businesses will moderate price increases if they do not expect inflation to accelerate in the future. This should also reduce the chance of 'second round effects' of rising oil prices on wages and retail prices. A **credible and transparent monetary framework** is crucial for the strategy to work.

(iii) It can provide a *nominal anchor* for monetary policy. In a monetary system where paper money is not backed by, say, gold, and the money itself is intrinsically worthless, there needs to be something to tie the price level down and keep it stable. As noted above, the money supply and the exchange rate have been used as nominal anchors in the past, but both failed.

(iv) Inflation targeting has worked in other countries. Examples include New Zealand in 1990 and Canada in 1991. New Zealand became the first country to formally adopt inflation targeting and its headline inflation fell from 8% in 1990 to 2% in 1998.

● Analysis: The transmission mechanism of monetary policy

Changes in interest rates affect inflation via their influence on aggregate demand in the economy. The transmission mechanism is complex and is summarised in Figure 9.1. A rise in interest rates, such as the rise from 4.5% to 5.75% between August 2006 and June 2007, could have the following effects on the economy:

(i) It increases the rate of return on saving and increase the cost of borrowing for consumers. This should lead to individuals saving more and spending less, since the **opportunity cost of spending has risen**. The demand for expensive consumer durables bought on credit such as widescreen TVs and PCs will decline.

(ii) For homeowners, a rise in interest rates will lead to higher interest repayments on mortgages. Homeowners will experience a fall in purchasing power as their real effective disposable income, or real income after housing costs, will have declined. Lower demand for housing will almost certainly lead to lower house prices, and since houses are a large part of personal wealth, the value of many individuals' wealth will fall, reducing consumer spending via the wealth effect.

(iii) Firms will also be affected by rising short term interest rates. This increases the cost of borrowing, reducing profits for firms with debt finance, reducing the marginal efficiency of capital, and therefore investment levels. Higher rates tend to reduce business confidence, or 'animal spirits'.

Figure 9.1: The transmission mechanism of monetary policy

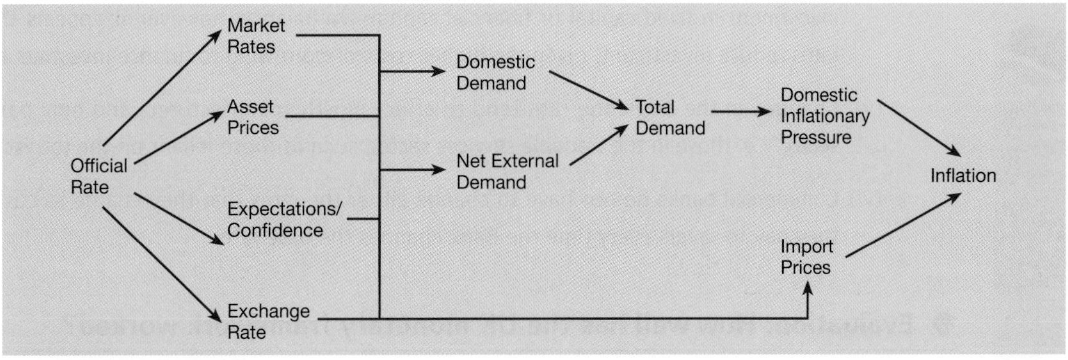

Source: www.bankofengland.co.uk

(iv) Higher interest rates might lead to a rise in the value of the pound. If UK rates rise above, say, dollar rates, the rate of return on holding pounds is higher than that on the dollar. This will attract speculative flows of **hot money**, raising the demand for pounds and so increasing the value of the pound. This has the effect of increasing the price of exports and reducing the price of imports. The consequent fall in export demand and rise in import demand is a leakage out of the circular flow, reducing aggregate demand and national income via the multiplier effect. Much 'hot money' ended up in Iceland in the mid 2000s, due to interest rates on the krona continually reaching record highs. Canny investors borrowed money in yen, on which interest rates were 0%, and put their money where rates were higher. This became known as the **yen carry trade**.

Extension material: Interest rates and share prices

There is an inverse relationship between interest rates and the price of bonds and equities (shares). The reason for this relationship is that the expected future returns will be discounted by a larger factor, lowering the present value of future income streams. Therefore rising interest rates will reduce the value of bonds and equities, lowering wealth and lowering spending. Higher interest rates also tend to depress consumer confidence, which contributes to lower consumer spending.

Question

3. Using an aggregate demand and aggregate supply diagram, analyse the likely impact on the price level and the equilibrium real level of output of a decision by the MPC to increase interest rates.

● Evaluation: The effects of a rise in interest rates

Forecasting the impact of higher interest rates is not easy for several reasons:

(i) There are considerable **time lags** involved as it takes about a year for changes in the repo rate to affect retail (commercial bank) rates and for this to affect aggregate demand, and about another year for changes in aggregate demand to affect inflation.

(ii) A rise in interest rates will not increase the cost of borrowing for those on fixed rate mortgages in the short term. However, they may be affected in the long run when the term of the fixed rate expires, and the terms of the mortgage need to be renegotiated.

(iii) Individuals with high levels of saving will find that their interest earnings increase, which they may well spend, increasing aggregate demand. However, for households as a whole the overall effect of higher interest rates appears to be reduced consumption and higher saving.

(iv) Similarly, some firms will receive higher income on their cash deposits which could lead to higher investment in fixed capital or financial capital. On balance, however, it appears that higher interest rates reduce investment, given the higher costs of borrowing to finance investment projects.

(v) Changes in the exchange rate tend to affect mostly manufacturers and only parts of the services sector, i.e. those in the tradable services sector, such as those reliant on the tourist trade.

(vi) Commercial banks do not have to change either the rates that they charge to customers or the rate they pay to savers every time the Bank changes the base rate.

● Evaluation: How well has the UK monetary framework worked?

Figure 9.2: The MPC's record in targeting the CPI

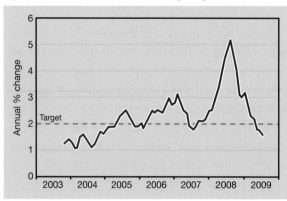

Source: ONS

Figure 9.3: UK CPI and Bank of England base rate 1999-2009

Source: ONS

In many ways, it would appear that the UK monetary framework since 1997 has been a success, especially compared to the turbulent period before then. The reasons are as follows:

• Inflation remained within its target range from the beginning of Bank of England independence in May 1997 right through to March 2007.

• In April 2001 the House of Commons Treasury Select Committee praised the MPC for establishing a high level of credibility.

• In 2004 the CPI was steadily rising towards its target of 2.0%. The MPC, clearly worried about future inflation, raised interest rates four times, from 3.75% in January 2004 to 4.75% by July 2004 as shown in Figure 9.3. It worked, as the CPI fell back below target by the end of 2005. There followed a remarkable period of stability during which interest rates were only changed once in two years.

• The MPC is well aware of its wider role in promoting UK growth and employment and is not simply made up of 'inflation nutters', a criticism often levelled at the European Central Bank, for example. In 2001, the Bank aggressively cut rates in order to choke off the threat of recession, and indeed 18-24 months later, in the latter half of 2002 and into 2003, inflation rose above and beyond its target. The Bank cut rates aggressively from 5% to 0.5% between October 2008 and March 2009, when it became apparent that the UK was about to enter recession.

However, there has also been reason to criticise the MPC at times:

• The House of Commons Treasury Select Committee, along with other commentators, believe that policy may have been biased towards undershooting the target. Between May 1999 and November 2002, inflation was continually below target for all but two months, suggesting that the committee may have been correct.

• Rising inflationary pressure in 2006 required five quarter point rises between August 2006 and June 2007. Figure 9.3 shows that the MPC may have reacted a little late to inflationary pressure: the blue line start to rise at the beginning of 2006, the red line not until August of that year.

In April 2007, it was announced that the CPI had breached its 3% target in March thus requiring the Governor of the Bank to write an open letter to the Chancellor explaining why this occurred and what would be done about it. This was the first time since Gordon Brown as Chancellor granted independence to the Bank in April 1997 that the Governor had suffered this ignominy. This was not the 10 year anniversary that the present governor, Mervyn King, was hoping for or expecting.

- The bursting of the UK housing bubble in 2007-9 has led to criticisms of the current 'one tool, one target' monetary framework. The CPI inflation target does not include asset prices such as house prices. It is very likely that both the Bank of England and the US Federal Reserve left interest rates too low for too long in the early 2000s. The Bank of England kept the CPI under control, but rapid house price inflation was evident for many years. The bursting of the bubble increases the risk of deflation in the medium term. This has led to criticism of the monetary framework of targeting consumer price inflation for the first time since its introduction in 1992. Some believe that asset price inflation should also be targeted. However, according to The Economist, it is unlikely that central bankers will abandon inflation targets as it would significantly reduce their credibility.[1] Neither, however, can they afford to ignore bubbles again!

Extension material: Quantitative easing

As mentioned in the last two chapters, the Bank reduced rates down to 0.5% by March 2009 in order to increase aggregate demand and stave off the threat of deflation. Interest rates had gone almost as low as possible, yet forecasts for UK GDP growth in 2009 remained dire, and the threat of deflation still lingered. This persuaded the Bank of England to try something new.

All commercial banks hold accounts with the Bank of England. **Quantitative easing** (QE) is when the Bank of England credits these accounts with more money. In return the banks sell various kinds of assets to the Bank of England: usually corporate bonds and government bonds. The size of the Bank of England's balance sheet expands, while that of the commercial banks reduces. If the banks want to keep the size of their balance sheets the same, they will lend out more money to customers. QE should have the same effect as 'printing money', although, in a modern economy, the central bank doesn't physically print more bank notes. The Bank of England pumped £200 billion of new liquidity (money) into the economy under its QE programme. The rise in demand for bonds from the Bank of England, and the fall in supply on the markets, should increase the price of bonds and reduce the interest rate on bonds, which is the benchmark for some fixed mortgage rates, bank overdraft rates and business borrowing. Remember, there is an inverse relationship between the price of bonds and the interest rate on bonds.

Arguments in favour of quantitative easing

(i) It should stimulate both the supply of credit, since banks want to maintain the size of their balance sheets, and the demand for credit, due to a fall in interest rates. This should stimulate aggregate demand and prevent deflation.

(ii) The Bank of England base rate has gone almost as low as it can go.

(iii) The policy could stimulate lending more directly, through the effects on fixed rate mortgages and business lending, than a fall in base rates could. However, banks may just add to their reserves and not lend the extra money.

(iv) It may have prevented recession in Japan between 2001-6.

Arguments against quantitative easing

(i) It could lead to inflation if it pumps too much money in the economy. However, the Bank can always

---

1. 'The monetary-policy maze', The Economist, 23 April 2009.

reverse the process – sell the bonds back to the market – as soon as inflation looks like it will go above target.

ii) If inflation gets out of control, it could lead to lenders refusing to lend the government more money. The pound would collapse on the foreign exchange markets, worsening the inflation problem.

iii) GDP growth in Japan was not particularly high in 2001-6, nor was it after its quantitative easing experiment ended. In fact it may have been the big rise in government spending, not QE, which prevented the Japanese economy from going into recession.

Extension material: The relationship between M4 and inflation

Figure 9.4: CPI and M4

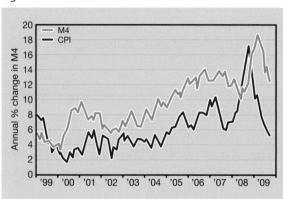

Source: ONS

Figure 9.4 compares the rate of growth of the CPI with the rate of growth of M4, which is the measure of broad money in the economy and is driven by bank lending.[2] Milton Friedman famously said that 'inflation is always and everywhere a monetary phenomenon' and historically the UK has shown a strong correlation between the rate of growth of the money supply and the rate of growth of prices. The Fisher Equation states that $MV = PT$, where M = Money Supply, V = Velocity of Circulation, P = Price Level, and T is Transactions or real output.

Given a constant V, a rise in the money supply must be accompanied by a rise in nominal GDP. However, V has varied considerably in the UK over the years, so clearly the relationship between money and nominal GDP is not straightforward.

Figure 9.4 shows that M4 growth accelerated between 2004 and 2007, and again towards the end of 2008. The Bank of England was initially concerned that this extra money may have been spent on assets, driving up the price of these assets, and leading to a rise in spending and inflation via the wealth effect. In fact, household lending has been relatively subdued: broad money growth has been concentrated in the holdings of OFCs (Other Financial Corporations), including pension and private equity funds. However, these are companies that intermediate funds between different banks who are thus not necessarily borrowing and spending lots of money in the conventional sense. Further, it may be that money is being borrowed and spent on assets abroad rather than in the UK economy. These factors may help to explain why broad money growth has been very rapid, but that inflation has not really followed suit. In 2008-9, M4 lending to households was below the rate of growth required to hit the 2% inflation target. This provides a further argument for quantitative easing. Thus it would seem that double digit growth in M4 will not lead directly to a commensurate rise in UK inflation.

Questions

4. Explain the effect of a 'boost in the supply of money' on inflation.

5. Assess the impact of the independence of the Bank of England on UK inflation since 1997.

---

2. Some of this material is from *Treasury enquiry into the Monetary Policy Committee of the Bank of England: Ten Years On*, at www.bankofengland.co.uk.

Chapter 10

UK Fiscal Policy

In this Chapter we examine recent changes in the UK tax system, trends in the pattern of government spending and the fiscal policy framework of the Labour government.

● Knowledge: Defining fiscal policy

Fiscal policy is when the government changes tax rates, government expenditure and borrowing to influence macroeconomic variables, such as aggregate demand. It also includes sources of government income other than taxes and assistance to the private sector such as tax breaks.

There are several objectives of fiscal policy:

(i)   To fund government spending.

(ii) To redistribute income and wealth more evenly.

(iii) A way of managing demand in the economy.

(iv) To influence the supply side of the economy via its effect on incentives and investment.

(v) To correct for negative externalities, such as pollution and passive smoking.

● Knowledge: Defining taxes

Figure 10.1: Breakdown of government tax revenue, 2009-2010, £bn (estimates)

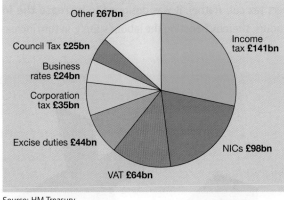

Source: HM Treasury

Direct taxes are taxes directly levied on individual incomes and company profits. They are paid directly to the exchequer by the individual or firm. The main examples in the UK are income tax, national insurance contributions (NICs), and corporation tax. A breakdown of government revenue in the financial year 2009-10 is given in Figure 10.1. By far the most important contributor to government revenue is income tax, followed by NICs. Most taxes in the UK are collected by HM Revenue and Customs. Council Tax and Business Rates are collected by local authorities.

Indirect taxes are taxes on expenditure. The most important indirect tax in terms of receipts is VAT as is apparent in Figure 10.1. Other examples include excise duties, customs duties, air passenger duty and the landfill tax. The crucial difference between direct and indirect taxes is that with direct taxes **the burden of the tax cannot be transferred onto any other party**. This is not the case with indirect taxes: for example, VAT is levied initially on the producer, who may then pass some of the burden of the tax onto the consumer.

Question

1. Which one of the following is NOT classified as fiscal policy?
   A. Fall in income tax.
   B. Printing bonds to finance a budget deficit.
   C. Raising government spending on the NHS.
   D. Raising interest rates.

● Application: UK tax revenues and tax rates

Table 10.1 shows the reduction in UK income tax rates since 1979.

Table 10.1: Changes in UK income tax rates

	Starting rate	Basic	Higher	New Top Rate
1979	–	33	83	–
1988	–	25	40	–
1992	25	25	40	–
1997	20	24	40	–
1999	10	22	40	–
2008	–	20	40	–
2011*	–	20?	40?	50

*Subject to government then in office

● Analysis: Income tax and tax credits

The reason for these income tax cuts was *not* to give a short term boost to aggregate demand, although this often occurs following a direct tax cut. Rather, it was designed to **increase the incentive to work**; to get individuals to work longer hours, thereby boosting the labour supply, in turn increasing the economy's trend rate of economic growth.

Tax cuts were designed to increase the incentive to work.

The Labour government has also changed the way that help is provided to poor families with the use of **tax credits** (see Chapter 4). This began with the introduction of the Working Families Tax Credit in 1999, and was replaced by a new Working Tax Credit in April 2003. The Working Tax Credit is a top up benefit paid to low income working families. The new Child Tax Credit is paid by HM Revenue and Customs directly to the main carer in the family and was introduced in 2003 in order to help tackle child poverty. Child Tax Credit is paid regardless of whether people work.

The idea behind the introduction, and subsequent lowering of, the starting rate of income tax and the new tax credits was to **make work pay** for poor households, since low income households often face very high marginal tax rates (the marginal rate of tax is the tax paid on the last pound earned) due to the withdrawal of benefit entitlement coupled with the obligation to pay tax. However, the abolition of the 10p starting rate in 2008 meant that childless single people earning under £18,500 a year could be worse off by up to £232/year, according to the House of Commons Treasury Committee. Those over the age of 25 were able to claim more generous tax credits, however.

Chancellor Alistair Darling announced in the 2009 Budget that there would be a new top rate of tax of 50% for those earning more than £150,000 as of 2011. The Treasury forecast that this would raise £6 billion between 2010/11 and 2012/13. The arguments in favour of the rise include:

- It would help to close the gap in the government's finances.

- It could help redistribute income from the rich to the poor.

- The money could be used to invest in public services.

The arguments against include:

- Individuals who are hit may reduce their spending, since their disposable income would fall. This would reduce the revenue from taxes on expenditure such as VAT.

- It acts as a disincentive to work, so less income will be earned, and less income tax taken.

- It may lead to individuals trying to avoid tax by converting income above £150,000 into capital gains.

- It may lead to a 'brain drain' as wealth-creating individuals seek to avoid tax by emigrating to places with lower tax regimes.

● Evaluation and extension material: Income and substitution effects

If income taxes are cut then the individual receives more post tax income for every hour worked. This will induce the individual to work longer hours and is known in the jargon as the **substitution effect**, since the individual substitutes work for leisure. The **income effect** works in the opposite direction. The individual may have a given target rate of post tax income in mind, and a cut in taxes means the individual has to work less hours to achieve that target level of income. This effect pulls the individual in the opposite direction and (s)he chooses to work less.

Theory alone cannot tell us which effect outweighs the other. Evidence from the Institute for Fiscal Studies suggests that, although incentives matter, the effect of change in income taxes on individuals depends on the type of individual.[1] Hours worked by males are almost entirely unresponsive, whereas hours worked by females are very responsive. Both male and female participation rates are highly responsive. On balance, cuts in direct taxes would seem to boost the incentive to work.

---

1. C. Meghir and D. Phillips 'Labour supply and taxes', Institute for Fiscal Studies, part of *Reforming the Tax System for the 21st Century*, The Mirrlees Review, IFS, (2009).

● Analysis: Corporation tax

The government has cut corporation tax rates in recent years in order to boost domestic fixed capital investment levels in the UK, and in order to attract foreign direct investment. It is also hoped that greater post tax profits will encourage UK firms to invest in research and development (R&D), an area where the UK has long lagged behind its major international competitors, to promote enterprise and innovation, and to ensure that the UK maintains and continues to attract high levels of foreign direct investment. As Chancellor Gordon Brown was very keen to reduce the **productivity gap** that the UK has with its major competitors that was discussed in Chapter 3.

Between 1997 and 1999, Chancellor Brown reduced the large company corporation tax rate from 33% to 30%. The 1999 Budget also saw a 1% cut in the small company rate to 20% and the introduction of a starting rate of corporation tax of 10%. In the 2002 Budget, the starting rate was reduced to 0% for companies earning £10,000 profit or less, and a further 1p cut was made in the starting rate to 19%. However, Brown later increased the small company rate to 21% and it is set to rise to 22% in 2010.

Figure 10.2: International comparison of corporate tax rates, %

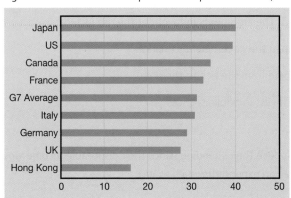

Source: PWC and www.worldwide-tax.com   The figures for Japan, US, Canada and Italy add 'local' or 'municipal' taxes to the 'headline' or 'federal rate' to get a better picture of the effective corporate tax rate.

The 2007 Budget saw a cut in the large company corporation tax rate by 2% to 28%, following reports that UK corporation tax was no longer at a low level compared to Europe. As Figure 10.2 shows, the UK's headline corporate tax rate is below that of its major competitors. Chancellor Gordon Brown has also introduced other tax incentives for investment. In the 2000 Budget he initiated permanent 40% capital allowances to encourage investment by small and medium sized firms and allowing small firms to write off 100% of their expenditure on ICT equipment against tax.[2] Since 2008, most businesses regardless of size have been able to claim a tax allowance on the first £50,000 of spending on plant and machinery.

Extension material: Capital gains tax

The government decided in 2007 to simplify greatly the capital gains tax system. The main rate was reduced from 40% to 18%, which means that when individuals sell shares or property, they now pay a much lower rate of tax. (Individuals don't have to pay capital gains tax when they sell their primary residence.) Under the old system, executives from **private equity companies** (see Chapter 3) only paid a tax rate of 10% on capital gains from selling a company, providing that they had owned that business for at least two years. This form of relief has now been abolished.

● ● Knowledge and Application: Tax rises

While there have been cuts in income tax and corporation tax, many taxes have risen in the UK in recent years. These include:

(i) The freezing of the thresholds at which people start paying higher rates of income tax and NICs. The thresholds went up by less than inflation on the RPI in 2000/01. In the Budget of 2002, the thresholds were frozen for the financial year 2003/4 in money terms. This raised many people's tax burden. In any

---

2. In fact, throughout the New Labour era, there have been various initiatives for small and medium sized businesses to claim tax allowances against spending on plant and machinery.

case, the thresholds rarely rise in line with the growth in average earnings, which was around 4-4.5% in the early and mid 2000s. More people got dragged into higher tax brackets, raising their tax burden. This is known as **fiscal drag**.

(ii) The rate of National Insurance contributions for employers and the self-employed was increased by 1% in 2003, increasing the employee rate to 11%, having been announced in the 2002 Budget. In the 2008 Pre-Budget Report, Chancellor Alistair Darling announced a further 0.5% increase in national insurance contributions for employers, employees and the self employed, which will apply from April 2011.

(iii) The introduction of new taxes, such as the landfill tax, a tax on the disposal of waste in landfill sites, in 1994, and in 2001 the climate change levy, a tax on business use of electricity, gas and coal. Other new taxes in the mid 1990s included insurance premium tax and airport passenger duty (APD).

(iv) There were significant increases in council tax bills in 2003 and 2004, although this rise was moderated in the election year of 2005, and the rise in council tax bills was much lower in 2006 and 2007. In 2004, the government announced a long-awaited revision of the council tax bands, which have existed since 1993. At the moment, the tax has highly **regressive** effects – it hits poorer households harder than rich ones – because the current bands made far more sense in 1993 than they do now. For example, the council tax bill for a house worth £320,000 today is exactly the same as the bill for a house worth £1 million in the same area! However, as yet this revision has not been implemented.

(v) Throughout the 1990s, excise duties on cigarettes, alcohol and tobacco were increased in real terms. Since 2000 tobacco duties have gone up in line with inflation, while alcohol duties have usually done so, with some exceptions – occasionally, certain duties have been frozen, and in 2008 all alcohol duties went up in real terms. The landfill tax was raised in the 2007 Budget by £8 per tonne per year, taking effect from April 2008, while the climate change levy was raised in line with inflation in each of the 2006-2008 Budgets. Fuel duty was increased in line with inflation in 2005 and 2006 and by 2p per litre in 2007 and 2009, but it will thereafter go up above inflation.

Question

2. The effect of higher average tax rates because taxpayers have moved into higher income brackets is called:
   A. Fiscal boost.
   B. Public sector net debt.
   C. Fiscal drag.
   D. Threshold drag.

● Analysis: Increases in excise duties

The economic reasons behind rising excise duties are:

• Demand for petrol, tobacco and alcohol is price inelastic, thus a modest rise in taxes will increase total revenue for the government. The resultant deadweight loss of economic welfare is lower for goods that have inelastic demand.

• They correct for the negative externalities generated by the overconsumption of tobacco, alcohol and petrol, and thereby reduce **market failure**.

The UK tax burden is shown in Figure 10.3 which clearly shows from 1993/4 to 2007/8 an upward trend. This was due to:

• The tax increases implemented by Chancellor Kenneth Clarke in the mid-1990s.

Figure 10.3: UK net tax and social security contributions as % GDP

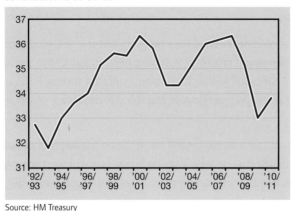

Source: HM Treasury

- New indirect or so-called 'stealth' taxes introduced by Gordon Brown since 1997.

- Rising employment levels which boosted income tax and NIC receipts.

The tax burden is forecast to decline to 33% by 2009-10, the lowest since 1994. This is because of the recession which will reduce receipts from income tax, NICs and also receipts from the housing and financial sectors. The standard rate of VAT was also reduced from 17.5% to 15% during the recession.

⬤ ⬤ Knowledge and Application: Government spending

Figure 10.4: Breakdown of UK government spending 2009-2010, £bn (estimates)

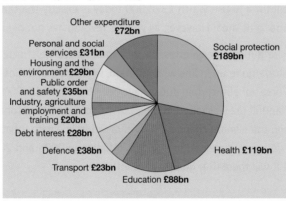

Source: HM Treasury

There is a distinction between two types of government expenditure. Public sector **current expenditure** is government expenditure on goods and services such as medicines and other recurring expenditure including public sector salaries. Public sector **capital expenditure** is government investment in infrastructure such as schools, hospitals, defence equipment, motorways and the rail network. It is capital spending that the government has been particularly keen to increase since 1998. The sum of these gives **Total Managed Expenditure** (TME).

The largest single item of government spending is not, as students commonly suppose, the NHS or education, but actually what is called social protection, as shown in Figure 10.4. This includes state pensions, Jobseekers Allowance and other social security benefits such as incapacity benefit.

⬤ Analysis of government spending trends

Figure 10.5: UK government spending figures

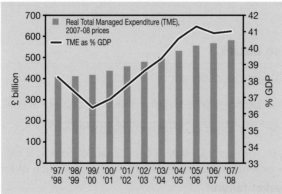

Source: HM Treasury

After the recession of the early 1990s, the Conservative government ended office with a large budget deficit. The Labour government in 1997 pledged an end to the days of large budget deficits and high national debt, and kept tight control of spending in the first two years of the administration as shown in Figure 10.5. By 1999/2000, TME as a % of GDP had fallen to 36.3% whereas the figure had been above 40% in the mid-1990s.

Between 2000 and 2006, however, Labour announced a series of boosts to government spending, especially in the areas of health and education (Figure 10.6), transport, housing, crime, defence and international development. This acted as a **Keynesian fiscal stimulus** to aggregate demand, and boosted UK GDP growth over the period. The biggest boost came in the 2002 Comprehensive Spending

Figure 10.6: UK government spending on health and education, current prices, £bn

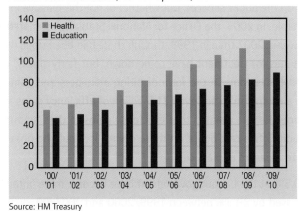

Source: HM Treasury

Review, which announced an annual average real increase in spending of 8.4% on transport, 8.1% on international development, 7.3% on health and 5.7% on education between 2002/3 and 2005/6. The 2004 Budget announced further significant rises in spending on the health service, so that by 2005/6 total NHS spending had reached £90bn, and that by 2008 UK spending on health would finally have reached the EU average. There were also big rises in spending on health and education announced in the 2004 Budget. Overall, public expenditure was raised by **well over £100 billion in real terms** between 2000/1 and 2006/7. Since 2006/7 growth in spending on many public services has been squeezed. This was always inevitable given the worsening state of the government's finances (discussed below).

Question

3. To what extent does the data in Figure 10.6 reflect accurately the growth in spending on health and education?

How successful has Brown's spending spree actually been?

The economic arguments for a rise in spending on the NHS are:

Rising life expectancies

UK life expectancy has risen on trend leading to an **ageing population**. Older people tend to be ill more often and also take a longer time to recover, increasing pressure on secondary health resources.

Increasing expectations

Higher living standards have led to rising consumer expectations from the health service. The demand for healthcare is highly **income elastic**.

Improvements in technology

A hip replacement operation is much more effective than a good bedside manner, but it also costs a lot more as well! The increased availability of treatments with the discovery of new drugs has meant that supply has created its own demand.

The crisis in the NHS

In 1997 the NHS was widely regarded to be in crisis as reflected in long waiting lists. The number of hospital beds had been falling for years and spending as a share of GDP was well below that of countries such as France and Germany.

The economic arguments for a rise in UK education spending are as follows:

- Rise in human capital, increasing the country's long term trend rate of economic growth.

- It will improve the UK's 'skills base', allowing the UK to improve productivity, and close the productivity gap with our competitors.

- In an ever more globalised and competitive world, where the premium attached to qualifications is rising, an educated workforce is essential in maintaining and improving the competitiveness of the UK economy and increasing living standards.

● Evaluation: Have things improved?

Labour may have spent billions on the public services, but whether or not this massive investment has been productive is certainly questionable. In 2009, the Office for National Statistics estimated that public sector output per worker was 3.2% *lower* in 2007 than in 1998, though there had been small rises in recent years. In the health service, waiting times for treatment have come down, but fairly slowly, while much of the boost to employment in the NHS has come in the form of hiring managers and administrative staff. In 2004, Chancellor Brown began a campaign to achieve £21.5 billion of efficiency gains in the public sector by 2007/8. The 2007 Pre Budget Report claimed that efficiency gains to date amounted to just £11.3 billion, though the National Audit Office cast doubt on these claims. It should be noted that efficiency is a notoriously difficult concept to measure in practice!

It would appear from Figure 10.5 that the Labour government have become more 'interventionist' as time has progressed. Real TME increased by 39.6% between 1999/2000 and 2007/08, or an average of 4.3% per year. However, even in 2007/8, following these huge rises in government spending, TME as a % of GDP was still lower than it was in the mid 1990s, under the Conservative administration. However, it should be noted that TME as a % of GDP is forecast to rise to 48% by 2010-11. In addition, the level of GDP in the mid-1990s was much lower than it was by 2007/8 after 15 years of uninterrupted economic growth. The worsening of the public finances meant that in the 2009 Budget, Chancellor Darling announced that real public spending would only rise by 0.7% per year.

●● Knowledge and Application: Government borrowing

Public sector net borrowing (PSNB) is the sum of government current spending and net investment, minus total government revenue each financial year. Public sector net debt, in contrast, is the total amount of debt owed by central and local government and public corporations.

Figure 10.7: UK public sector borrowing as % GDP

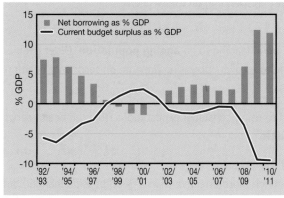

Source: HM Treasury

Figure 10.7 illustrates that in the mid 1990s the PSNB was very high following the long and deep recession of the early 1990s. Thereafter, strong economic growth and falling unemployment boosted income tax revenues, while the Conservative and Labour governments kept a strict control on public spending throughout the 1990s. This meant that between 1998/9 and 2000/01 the government was able to repay debt. However, since then government borrowing has increased once more, partly because economic growth has been slightly weaker, but mainly due to the rapid rise in spending of the central government on health and education as shown in Figure 10.6.

The **cyclically adjusted** PSNB adjusts for the effects of the economic cycle on government borrowing, in other words what government borrowing would be if there were no variations in the business cycle, or GDP. Figure 10.8 indicates that there is a

Figure 10.8: Cyclically adjusted government borrowing figures as % GDP

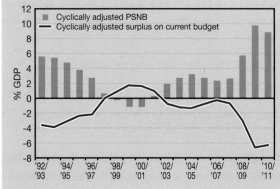

Source: HM Treasury

structural deficit here as there was a deficit during both periods of economic growth (2000-2007) and recession (2008-9).

● Analysis: Is the PSNB a problem?

A PSNB can be problematic for the following reasons:

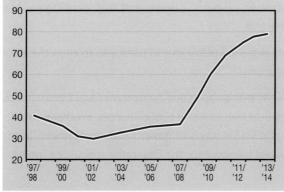

Figure 10.9: UK public sector net debt as % GDP

Source: HM Treasury

• In the long run, successive years of borrowing add to public sector net debt. Note the soaring debt as a proportion of GDP after 2007 as shown in Figure 10.9.

• It may lead to a rise in the tax burden in the future.

• It may lead to 'crowding out effects'. This is where the government finances a PSNCR by issuing government **bonds**, or long term government debt. Interest rates may have to go up in the medium term to make purchase of the bonds attractive, **crowding out** private sector investment. In fact, long term bond yields have generally remained low in recent years.

A PSNB can be beneficial because:

• It raises aggregate demand and boosts GDP levels. There is no doubt that UK economic growth would have been substantially less were it not for the boost in government current and capital spending.

• Government capital spending boosts the supply side, and raises the productive potential of the economy, hopefully increasing long run aggregate supply, and economic growth.

Question

4. Explain the difference between the PSNB and public sector net debt.

● Analysis: Why have the UK government's finances worsened since 2000-01?

• Large real increases in government spending on public services 2000-7 signalling an end to the tight control earlier dubbed 'prudence' by Chancellor Brown.

• Rising levels of unemployment since 2006. Spending on Job Seekers' Allowance (JSA) for the unemployed has risen as a result. This is known as an **automatic stabiliser**: when unemployment rises, spending on JSA will rise automatically without any change in government policy.

• Lower than expected tax revenues in the mid 2000s.

• The recession in 2008-9. The recession significantly reduced tax revenues, especially in the financial sector. Lower consumer spending reduced VAT receipts, lower incomes reduced income tax and NICs, while lower company profits reduced corporation tax receipts.

• Financial sector rescues: direct support for banks such as Northern Rock, Bradford and Bingley and Lloyds Banking Group.

●● Knowledge and Application: Labour's fiscal policy framework – the end of prudence

Under the Conservative government of 1979-97, current expenditure was consistently in excess of current revenue, and thus there were budget deficits. In 1993/4 the PSNCR reached £50 billion, or 7.1% of GDP. This led to a steady decline in net public sector wealth. When Labour took office in 1997, they were keen not to repeat the mistakes of the Conservatives, so they designed a new fiscal policy framework.

The new Government's fiscal policy objectives were:

- 'Over the medium term, to ensure sound public finances and that spending and taxation impact fairly within and between generations; and

- Over the short term, to support monetary policy and, in particular, to allow the automatic stabilisers to help smooth the path of the economy.'[3]

The idea behind the first objective is that an *open and transparent fiscal framework* coupled with careful control of government spending would lead to sound public finances, in other words no unsustainable rise in the national debt, and high and stable levels of growth and employment. In accordance with the government's desire for openness and transparency, the Chancellor announced two key fiscal rules in order to achieve this objective.

- **The Golden Rule**: This rule stated that the government should borrow only to invest and not to fund current spending. Over the period 1998/9 to 2001/2, when the economy was growing above trend, the current budget was in surplus. However, it did go into deficit in 2002/3, where it has remained ever since. This did not contravene the golden rule, however, as the government had to **balance the current budget on average over the economic cycle**. However Chancellor Brown kept changing his assessment of when the current economic cycle started and finished! He said in 2004 that the current economic cycle began in 1999 and would end in 2005. But this would have meant that he would have not kept to the golden rule and he would have missed it by just over £5 billion. The Budget Report for 2007, however, established the cycle as starting in 1997 and ending at the beginning of 2007. On these assumptions, the Treasury claims that between 1997/8 and 2006/7 there was an average annual surplus on the current budget of 0.1%. Brown's critics, on the other hand, accused him of breaking the Golden Rule in 2006.

The recession of 2008-9 meant a steep decline in the current budget, as shown by the dip in the purple line in Figure 10.7 – a clear breaking of the Golden Rule. The government had not expected such a severe recession, or such a severe worsening of its finances. They went back to a more 'Keynesian' fiscal policy of cutting tax rates, such as the VAT cut, and raising government spending. The government effectively scrapped the Golden Rule in 2008.

- **The Sustainable Investment Rule** was that public sector net debt as a proportion of GDP would be held at a stable and prudent level, which the government stated to be 40% of GDP. The acceleration in PSNB after 2007 has significantly added to the national debt, and will see it rise to nearly 80% by 2013-14 as Figure 10.9 shows. There was no possibility of keeping the figure anywhere near 40%, so this rule was also scrapped in 2008.

● Evaluation: Has the government managed the public finances well?

After beginning 'prudently', Gordon Brown left the post of Chancellor with a reputation of one who had 'spent, taxed and borrowed too much'. He did leave the Exchequer in 2007 with the public finances in a better state than when he took office some ten years previously. However, the subsequent worsening of the government's finances under his premiership during 2008-09 leave his legacy to say the least as a prudent economic manager in serious doubt. The budget deficit as a share of GDP will be higher than in

---

3. HM Treasury, Budget 2009.

Figure 10.10: International comparison of central government debt 2008, % GDP

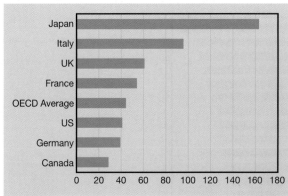

Source: OECD

the last recession, so too public sector net debt, and both fiscal rules have been scrapped. National debt as a share of GDP is now well above the average for OECD nations as is shown in Figure 10.10. The reasons for the recession were, to a great degree, out of the government's hands (see Chapter 1). However, there is a broad consensus amongst many commentators that the government could and should have saved more during the years of economic growth.

Question

5. Expansionary fiscal policy is most likely to cause:
   A. A rise in unemployment?
   B. A worsening of the current account balance?
   C. A fall in import volumes?
   D. A fall in the rate of inflation?

●● Application and Analysis: International comparison of public finances

Figure 10.11: Forecast government spending as % GDP 2009

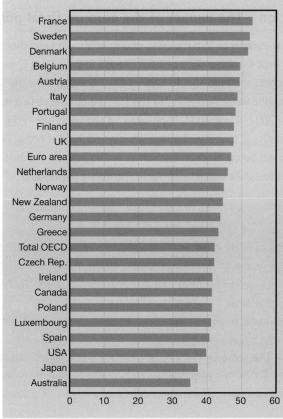

Source: OECD

Traditionally, the UK is thought of as a middle ranked country in terms of the size of the state's involvement in the economy. However, Figure 10.11 shows that currently the UK is just above the euro area average and well above the OECD average, further evidence of the Labour government's interventionist approach. Government spending accounts for a much greater share of GDP than 'free market' economies such as the US, but a lower share than more 'mixed economies' that have a 'high tax, high spend' model such as the Scandinavian countries. It is also true that the state's share of the economy has increased in most other developed economies since the 1960s.

The UK is often seen as a high tax nation, and that this reduces our economic growth rate. In fact the UK is a middle-ranked country in terms of its tax burden as shown in Figure 10.12. The UK in 2009 was just above the OECD average, but below the Euro area average. The tax burden is below the 'statist' countries such as Scandinavia and 'Old Europe', such as France and Germany, but above more free market economies such as the US.

Figure 10.12: Forecast tax and non tax receipts as % GDP 2009

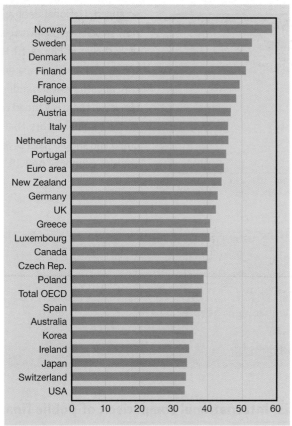

Source: OECD

● ● Knowledge and Application – The impact of the euro on fiscal policy

In 1992, EU countries agreed that in order to join the euro, countries should keep their budget deficits to within 3% of GDP, and national debt to within 60% of GDP. The EU Stability and Growth Pact, agreed in 1997, meant that countries adopting the euro should balance their budgets over the business cycle and aim for a budget deficit of 3% GDP or less. According to the EU, the budget deficit in the UK exceeded 3% of GDP two years running, in 2003/4 and 2004/5; however, as the UK is not in the eurozone, it could not be fined. Of course, the figure is set to rise well above 3% beyond 2008. Gordon Brown has criticised the Stability and Growth Pact for not being 'flexible' enough as during periods of economic slowdown and rising unemployment, countries need their budget deficits to rise above the ceiling.

Questions

6. Assess the economic effects of a rise in government spending as a share of GDP.
7. Evaluate the effects of a rise in the UK tax burden on the UK economy.
8. Examine the effects on the economy of running a balanced budget, in line with the UK government's fiscal policy objectives.
9. Evaluate the impact on the UK economy of the rise in PSNB from 2.5% of GDP to 12% of GDP from 2007/8 to 2009/10, as shown in Figure 10.7.
10. To what extent might UK membership of the euro affect UK fiscal policy?

Chapter 11

European Issues

The position of the UK within the EU has been a huge source of controversy down the years. Debates regarding European economic and social issues seem rarely to be out of the headlines. This Chapter examines four crucial European economic issues:

• The Single European Market, together with EU competition policy.

• European Monetary Union (EMU).

• EU enlargement, along with the issue of immigration.

• The Common Agricultural Policy.

Before examining this controversy surrounding these issues we briefly contrast the performance of the EU economy with that of the UK.

● ● Knowledge and Application: UK vs. EU comparative statistics

Table 11.1 provides some simple comparative statistics between the UK and Euro Area. It is clear that the UK macroeconomy generally outperformed that of the Euro area over the last ten years.

Table 11.1: UK and the Euro Area – selected statistics

	UK	EU27	EU15
Average Annual GDP growth 1999-2008 (%)	2.6	2.3	2.2
Average LFS Unemployment rate 2008 (% labour force)	5.22	8.4*	7.69
Average Inflation Rate 1999-2008 (%)	1.8	2.2	2.7
Average Short Term Interest Rate 1999-2008 (%)	5.0	3.8[†]	–

Source: OECD   *Figures are for 2000-2008   [†]Figures are for 2001-2008

Figure 11.1: UK and EU15 GDP growth

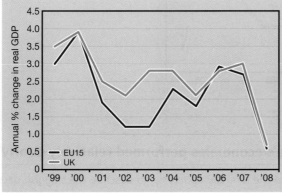

Source: OECD

• UK economic growth was slightly stronger and a little more stable than in the EU as shown in Figure 11.1.

• Unemployment has been lower in the UK, though EU unemployment began to move towards that of the UK between 2004 and 2008 as shown in Figure 11.2.

• Despite the recent rise in UK inflation, the UK outperformed the Euro area over the last ten years, (Figure 11.3) although UK interest rates have had to stay consistently above that of the Euro area, as Figure 11.4 makes clear, in order to achieve this.

Figure 11.2: LFS unemployment in EU15 and selected countries

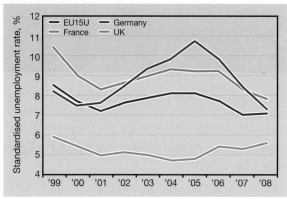

Source: OECD

Figure 11.3: UK and EU 15 inflation

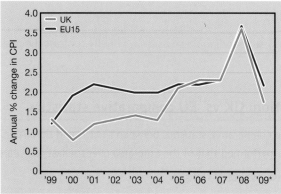

Source: OECD   *Forecast

Figure 11.4: Bank of England and European Central Bank base rates

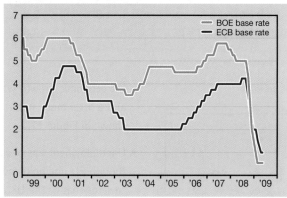

Source: OECD

The recession of 2008-09 has changed the picture somewhat. UK economic growth has collapsed and was forecast to be -3.7% in 2009, while growth in the Euro Area will be even worse, at -4.1%.[1] Unemployment rose quickly in the UK in 2008-09, but was still 2% below that of the Euro Area as of June 2009.

The UK is a net contributor to the EU to the extent of £4.2bn in 2005 – about £70 a head. This is partly because the UK is a net contributor to the Common Agricultural Policy (CAP, discussed below), but also because it is one of the countries in the EU with a relatively high GDP.

Question

1. Explain the reason for the differences in the unemployment rates shown in Figure 11.2.

● Analysis: Why have Europe's economies performed relatively poorly?

In the 1980s, economists coined the term *'eurosclerosis'* to describe the sluggish pace of the European economy. France, Germany and Italy are still criticised for:

• Lack of innovation and research and development (R&D).

• Regulation that stifles entrepreneurship: it takes longer to start up a company in France and Germany compared to the UK and US and there are more forms to fill in.

1. Source: Economist's Poll Forecast.

- High taxes, especially in the Scandinavian countries, France and Belgium (see Chapter 10), though Germany has reduced its tax burden recently).

- A heavily regulated labour market (see below).

- A slower take up of ICT investment than the UK and US.

- Although the euro has boosted intra-EU trade, some countries such as Italy have not been able to allow their currencies to depreciate and restore competitiveness.

However, Euro Area GDP growth was slightly above the UK's in 2006 and Figure 11.1 clearly shows that the growth lines have now converged. In addition, much of the UK's GDP growth has been down to large increases in consumer borrowing and spending, rather than any substantial improvement in innovation and productivity.

Unemployment in the EU has remained above that of the UK for several reasons:

(i)   There is less **cyclical unemployment** in the UK, because the UK emerged from the early 1990s recession before Europe and because since then economic growth has been higher in the UK than in the EU.

(ii) The UK has managed to attract a significant amount of foreign direct investment (FDI) into the country, especially into the City of London.

(iii) Labour market flexibility is reckoned to be greater in the UK than in the rest of the EU. Trade unions are more powerful in France and Germany and unemployment benefits relatively more generous. It is easier to hire and fire labour in the UK, leading to more job creation, and the lack of trade union power means less industrial action and more wage flexibility.

● Evaluation: EU countries are starting to implement structural labour market reforms

(i)   Germany has made it harder to obtain unemployment benefit, made wage bargaining more flexible and reduced social security contributions, thereby reducing the cost of employing labour.

(ii) EU tax rates have been reduced, such that the UK corporation tax was now higher than the average for the EU15 until the headline rate was cut in the Budget of 2007.

(iii) Greater migration from Eastern Europe has also improved labour market flexibility. When demand for labour in Ireland was high in the early 2000s, for example, there were many Eastern European migrants offering their labour to meet rising demand. However, it is expected that the 2008-9 recession will cause some of these workers to leave, thus reducing the unemployment rate.

It should also be noted that Denmark, Italy and Austria all have lower unemployment than the UK.

Since the launch of the Euro in 1999, the UK has managed to keep inflation below that of the Euro Area at least until 2006, when the UK CPI was just higher than the Euro Area. This has not prevented interest rates in the UK from being persistently higher, however as is shown in Figure 11.4. The reasons for this are that actual GDP is operating closer to **potential** in the UK than in the EU, so the potential for demand pull inflation is higher. In addition, the Bank of England has been concerned about the housing boom, which has been more pronounced in the UK than in Europe.

● Knowledge: The Single European Market

The Single European Market (SEM) is a **common market**. That means that there is free movement of goods and services between EU member states with a **common external tariff**. The tariff applied to imports from outside the EU must be the same for each member state so that, for example, if Germany has a 10% tariff on Japanese car imports, then the UK must also apply the same tariff. It also means that there should be free movement of labour and capital throughout the EU.

The SEM came into being with the onset of the Single European Act, which came into force on 1st July 1987. The idea was to remove all trade barriers by 1992 so that the SEM could formally come into existence on 1st January 1993. This includes not just tariffs and quotas but also establishing common hygiene rules, common quality and health and safety standards and abolishing restrictive public procurement policies (government purchases of goods, services and other supplies from the private sector) delivering better value and higher quality services for the taxpayer.

The development of the EU: a timeline

1952:	Creation of European Coal and Steel Community
1957:	Treaty of Rome signed, creating the European Economic Community (EEC)
January 1958:	EEC formally comes into existence, comprising Germany, France, Italy, Belgium, Netherlands, Luxembourg
1962:	Establishment of the CAP
1973:	UK, Republic of Ireland and Denmark join EEC
1981:	Greece joins EEC
1986:	Spain and Portugal join. EEC becomes the EC
July 1987:	Single European Act comes into force. Outline includes objectives for a single market and single currency
February 1992:	Maastrict Treaty signed. UK opts out of EMU and the Social Charter
January 1993:	Creation of the Single European Market. EC becomes the EU
January 1995:	Austria, Finland, Sweden join
January 1999:	Single European Currency launched
January 2002:	Euro notes and coins first issued to public
May 2004:	Ten CEEC economies accede: Czech Republic, Cyprus, Estonia, Hungary, Latvia, Lithuania, Malta, Poland, Slovakia and Slovenia
29th May 2005:	EU constitution rejected by France and the Netherlands
1st January 2007:	Romania and Bulgaria join EU

● Analysis: Advantages of SEM

(i) The SEM allows member states to reap the benefits of free trade that arise according to the law of comparative advantage. This states that countries that specialise and trade in the goods and services in which they have a relative cost advantage will enjoy consumption of all goods and services in larger quantities and therefore enjoy higher living standards.

● Evaluation: Trade creation and diversion

In reality, the SEM has led to both trade creation and trade diversion effects. **Trade creation** occurs when countries move from competing with a high-cost producer to competing with a low-cost producer. The UK's second biggest single trading partner is Germany, and following the creation of the SEM, UK consumers and producers can purchase German imports tariff free, and vice versa. This should stimulate greater trade, hence the term trade creation. **Trade diversion** is the opposite: when a country moves from trading with a low-cost producer to trading with a high-cost producer. After the UK joined the EU, New Zealand lamb, for example, became much more expensive in the UK as it became subject to the common external tariff. Consumers switched towards lamb imports from EU countries that were not subject to the tariff, but that had a higher factor cost. Studies of the founding six members of the EU, for NAFTA (North American Free Trade Area) and the European Free Trade Area suggest that the trade creation effects just outweigh the trade diversion effects, and hence that the SEM should increase living standards.

(ii) The SEM should lead to more intense competition between EU firms, as under a single market they are now competing on a more level playing field. The move towards a more competitive EU market should, according to economic theory, lead to an increase in **static efficiency**. Static efficiency is concerned with efficiency at a point in time. There are two types: **productive efficiency**, which exists when production takes place at the minimum possible average cost, and **allocative efficiency**, which is concerned with whether resources are allocated to produce the goods and services that consumers wish to buy, and occurs when production takes place at the marginal cost of production. The effects of competition should drive down prices, increasing consumer welfare.

(iii) The effects of competition would lead to **price convergence**, as arbitrage would lead to the erosion of price differentials. Arbitrage is where people buy up the good in low price areas and sell it in high price areas.

● **Evaluation: Convergence in practice?**

At the time of writing, however, the evidence for price convergence is rather limited, and major price differentials still exist between member states for products as diverse as automobiles and iTunes downloads as Tables 11.2 and 11.3 show.

Table 11.2: iTunes: pricing per download

UK	79p
Denmark	72p
Germany	66p
France	66p
Belgium	66p

Source: Research by *Which?* cited at http://news.bbc.co.uk

Table 11.3: Car prices – difference in % terms between cheapest and most expensive country, selected automobile models

Renault Clio	16%
Peugeot 206	19.8%
VW Golf	24.3%
Ford Focus	28.8%
BMW 320D	5.5%
Ford Mondeo	24.6%

Source: www.europa.eu

(iv) Successful firms, with access to a potential market of nearly half a billion consumers, should be able to exploit economies of scale.

(v) The SEM should lead to gains in **dynamic efficiency**, which is concerned with how efficiently resources are allocated over time. Knowledge spillovers, the diffusion of information about new products and new processes, should occur due to the elimination of all barriers to trade, including legal barriers.

The above analysis is of the microeconomic benefits of the SEM, the benefits that accrue to firms and consumers. The macroeconomic benefits were reckoned to be:
• Stronger GDP growth.
• Lower unemployment.
• Lower inflation.
• Higher productivity.

● **Evaluation: The overall effects of the SEM**

In 1988 the Cecchini Report forecast that there would be a one-off rise in EU GDP of between 4.5% and 6.5%, a fall in unemployment of up to 1.5%, price deflation of 6.1% and an improvement in member states' external and budget balances. In fact, although GDP did rise and unemployment fell, the initial effects were somewhat muted compared to the forecasts. The OECD concluded in 1994 that the SEM

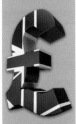

programme did not have sizeable effects on EU output. One reason why the Commission's estimates may have exaggerated the benefits is that they were based around the theories of perfect competition and comparative advantage, which have simplistic assumptions and are subject to criticism. Most major markets in EU member states are dominated by oligopolies producing branded products.

More recent data from the European Commission concluded that between 1993 and 2003 the single market created 2.5 million new jobs and generated more than €800 billion in extra wealth. Undoubtedly the single market has been a success in some respects: there is free movement of goods within the EU, people can go to study, to work or retire in another country easily and prices have plummeted in sectors such as low cost airlines, telecommunications and broadband internet access. Financial markets have become much more closely integrated, so that it now costs a lot less to transfer money across borders in the EU, and it is much easier, and costs consumers a lot less, to use credit and debit cards while abroad.

Question

2. Explain the benefits to the UK of membership of the SEM.

In March 2000, when the EU and global economic outlook was particularly favourable, EU leaders met at a summit in Lisbon and devised the Lisbon Agenda. The idea was to invigorate economic reforms and further deregulate EU markets, in order to make the EU a more dynamic and competitive knowledge based economy. The EU leaders planned the following:

• To make ICT as accessible to as many people as possible.

• To raise productivity in education and research.

• To make the EU more competitive, with specific focus on the service sector, such as the deregulation of the gas, electricity, postal and transport services.

• Increased coordination of EU financial markets.

• The reinforcement of macroeconomic stability in the EU: EU leaders set a target of 3% annual GDP growth and the creation of 20 million jobs by 2010.[2]

Figure 11.1 suggests there was not much progress in the short term as EU growth fell between 2000 and 2004, and structural unemployment remained high. Recovery from the slowdown of the early 2000s was slower for the EU than for the UK and US. The Lisbon Agenda was clearly in need of a relaunch. The European Commission had previously launched the Services Directive which was a plan to reduce further barriers to trade in services as diverse as hotels and restaurants, car hire, architecture, construction, estate agencies and the legal profession. The problem is that France and Germany did not welcome the directive as warmly as countries such as the UK. They pointed towards the 'country of origin' principle, which states that if a company was operating outside its country of origin, it would operate under the rules and regulations of its own country, not the country it was working in. Some trade unions said that this could lead to an overall reduction in standards, and a so-called 'race to the bottom' where companies would relocate production to countries with more lax regulation and standards.[3] 2005 turned out to be a bad year for the EU, as France and the Netherlands rejected the constitution in a referendum. The Services Directive was finally adopted by the European Parliament and the Council in December 2006. However, the country of origin principle has been replaced by a 'country of destination' principle, so companies operating abroad will have to adhere to the rules and regulations of the countries they are operating in.

2. See www.europa.eu
3. See 'Q&A: Eu's Lisbon Agenda' on http://news.bbc.co.uk

The single European market has created 2.5 million new jobs between 1993 and 2003.

Mergers and Acquisitions

Figure 11.5: Merger activity in the EU

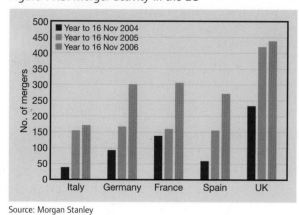

Source: Morgan Stanley

One undoubted effect of the SEM was a growth in cross-border mergers and acquisitions in the mid to late 1990s, inevitable given the elimination of barriers to the movement of factors of production and financial capital. There was a further explosion of cross-border takeovers in the mid 2000s as shown in Figure 11.5, led by the UK. At the time of writing, Germany and others are trying to implement legislation that would make it more difficult for foreign companies to take over companies deemed to be 'strategically important', such as in the energy sector.

● ● Knowledge and Application: Competition policy

A free market economy cannot function unless the government acts to promote the workings of the price mechanism through competition policy. Critical to the functioning of the Single European Market, therefore, is an EU wide **competition policy**. There are two main competition rules set out in the EC Treaty.

(i) **Article 81** prohibits anticompetitive practices such as price fixing, limiting production, sharing markets or sources of supply, restrictive practices and exclusive dealing. If such practices are discovered, they are often punished with fines. In 2005, four Italian tobacco firms were fined a total of €56 million for price collusion between 1995 and 2002. 2007 saw the largest EU fine ever imposed, on the German firm ThyssenKrupp, of €479.7 million. ThyssenKrupp was operating a cartel with three other companies in the market for the installation and maintenance of lifts and escalators in Belgium, Germany, Luxembourg and the Netherlands. These firms informed each other of calls for tender and co-ordinated

their bids according to pre-agreed cartel quotas. The other three companies were fined smaller amounts than ThyssenKrupp, as this firm was a repeat offender.

(ii) **Article 82** is concerned with abuse of a dominant position by one firm or a group of firms with monopoly power. This includes predatory pricing and limit pricing, and limiting production, for example through the use of quotas. If companies are found to have abused their dominant position, they may be fined up to 10% of their turnover. The EU authorities also have the right to raid a company's premises in search of evidence!

Mergers may also be investigated if the EU believes they will threaten competition and create monopoly power. Businesses must notify the European Commission if the proposed merger leads to EU and worldwide sales in excess of specific thresholds. Sometimes the Commission will allow the merger to go ahead, provided that the businesses concerned agree to certain measures that will restore competition. This occurred in the case of two mergers between pharmaceutical companies, Sanofi/Synthélabo in 1998 and Pfizer/Pharmacia in 2002-3. In both cases, the two firms agreed to transfer some of their products in development to competitors, and both mergers went ahead. In other cases, such as the proposed merger between General Electric and Honeywell in 2001, the Commission may block the merger.[4]

UK competition policy has been closely modelled on that of the EU. Chapter 1 of the 1998 Competition Act prohibits anti competitive agreements and restrictive practices by firms, while Chapter 2 of the Act prohibits the abuse of a dominant position in the UK market. (Chapter 3).

● Knowledge: The Single European Currency

We turn now away from the SEM including competition policy to consider the introduction of the euro. The Single European Currency was launched on the 1st January 1999. Eleven of the fifteen EU members initially joined the single currency with Greece joining in 2001.

Belgium
Austria
France
Finland
Luxembourg
Ireland
Netherlands
Germany
Portugal
Italy
Greece
Spain   ...which spells out **BAFFLING PIGS**!

More recently, Slovenia joined in 2007, Cyprus and Malta in January 2008 and Slovakia in January 2009. Sweden was judged not to have met the convergence criteria, while the UK and Denmark both opted out.

In order to qualify for EMU membership, each country has to meet the convergence criteria laid down under the Maastrict Treaty of February 1992:

• A country's inflation rate (HICP) should not exceed more than 1.5% of the average of the best (i.e. lowest) three performing nations.

• A country's interest rate on long term government bonds should not exceed 2% of the average of the three best (i.e. lowest) performing nations.

---

4. http://ec.europa.eu

- The budget deficit should be no more than 3% of GDP and the national debt should be no more than 60% of GDP.

- The nation's currency must have been semi-fixed inside the Exchange Rate Mechanism (ERM) for at least two years prior to entry.

In practice, some countries have been allowed to join without strictly adhering to all of the criteria. For example, Italy's national debt was higher than 60% of GDP, but because it was falling rapidly towards this figure in the late 1990s, they were allowed to join.

Extension material: Are the criteria helpful?

More recently the fiscal policy criteria have come under intense criticism as first Germany and France and now the UK have recently missed these criteria. This has led commentators to view the criteria as arbitrary and preventing governments from using fiscal policy to smooth out fluctuations in the business cycle. It should also be noted that the criteria are very 'monetarist' or 'neoclassical' in nature, taking as their premise the idea that interest rate and exchange rate policy will only affect monetary variables and not real variables. The UK is neither meeting the fiscal policy criteria, nor is it a member of ERM II, although the exchange rate has been sufficiently stable and the criteria sufficiently flexible that the UK would probably have no problem in joining should the government decide to do so.

●● Analysis and Evaluation:
The potential advantages for the UK joining the single currency

There are several arguments about the desirability of the UK adopting the euro which we consider in turn.

(i) Elimination of transactions costs
For many, the single currency is a logical extension of the single market, as the only remaining barriers to trade, the commission charges incurred when changing currencies, and the risk factor of currencies changing in value, will be eliminated. This will be advantageous for firms and consumers alike as it will increase the efficiency of intra EU transactions. However, this is only a 'one-off' gain, estimated as a rather modest 0.4% of EU GDP.

(ii) Reduction of exchange rate uncertainty
At the moment, UK firms face uncertainty when they trade with Europe as the price they receive for their exports and the price they pay for imports may change after signing a contract. Entry into the euro would end this uncertainty and probably increase trade, investment and output in the UK economy. However, the same certainty could be gained by keeping the pound and pegging it to the euro. Firms can also hedge against uncertainty by buying and selling currencies on the futures markets, although there are charges for this. Small firms will therefore benefit particularly from the reduction in exchange rate uncertainty. In addition, of course, uncertainty between the euro and other major currencies such as the dollar will still exist. This is particularly important for the UK as the US is our biggest trading partner.

(iii) Price transparency
Joining the euro means that UK businesses and consumers will be easily able to compare the price of the same goods and services in different countries. This might further enhance the arbitrage effects discussed above and lead to price convergence. However, cross border shopping would have to increase substantially from current levels for this to really occur in the UK, and in any case price differentials will still exist due to differences in indirect taxes, unit labour costs and so on.

However, opponents to the single currency point to the following counter arguments to the UK adopting the euro:

(i) Loss of sovereignty

The most common argument against adoption of the euro is that the UK would have to surrender monetary and exchange rate policy to the European Central Bank in Frankfurt. Interest rates in the UK would no longer be set with regard solely to UK economic objectives, but to the whole of the Eurozone. The fact that the UK and EU business cycles have not yet fully converged means that the ECB might set an interest rate that is appropriate for the rest of the Eurozone, but inappropriate for the UK. This is a particularly sensitive issue for the UK economy, given that firstly, a greater proportion of the population own their own home in the UK compared to most of Europe, and secondly, that more mortgage lending is on variable interest rates than in the Eurozone. Already there is evidence that the ECB's 'one size fits all' interest rate has met with problems, such as in 2000-1 when the Irish economy was overheating but the rest of Europe was growing very slowly. Italy, as mentioned above, has suffered a lack of competitiveness from being unable to devalue.

(ii) Inflationary problems

Many consumers have claimed that the introduction of the euro allowed businesses to take advantage of the confusion of getting used to a new currency by increasing the prices of goods such as groceries and restaurant meals. The official statistics, however, state that the circulation of euro notes and coins only increased Eurozone inflation by 0.2%.

(iii) Menu costs

The costs for businesses and banks of changing price lists from sterling into euros. These costs will fall most heavily on small and medium-sized businesses, but again it should be noted that these are once and for all costs.

(iv) Structural problems

A region can cope with a single currency if it has the following three characteristics: wage flexibility, labour mobility, and an efficient way of transferring revenue from taxes to declining regions that require assistance. In other words, if the region is hit by economic shocks, and monetary policy cannot ease these shocks, then wages must adjust, labour migrate, or financial resources transferred to the countries that require them. Whilst this may be true to an extent between the six founding members of the EU: Germany, France, Italy and the Benelux countries, very few commentators would argue that it is true of the entire Eurozone.

● Knowledge: The European Central Bank and the Bank of England

How does the European Central Bank differ from the UK's Central Bank? Here are some comparisons:

(i) The inflation target for the European Central Bank (ECB) is non symmetrical: <2% growth in CPI. The Bank of England (BOE) needs to hit a symmetrical inflation target (see Chapters 8-9), but also has the wider mandate of meeting the government's objectives for employment and growth.

(ii) The ECB also targets the rate of growth of the money supply, which the BOE does not.

(iii) The ECB was accused of being too anti inflationary at the expense of growth under its former president Wim Duisenburg. This reputation still exists despite more aggressive rate cuts under the new president Jean-Claude Trichet. For example, in response to the threat of recession, the Bank of England cut rates from 5% to 0.5% between July 2008 and March 2009. In contrast, the ECB **raised** rates in July to 4.25%, but has since cut rates to 1.5%.

(iv) The BOE is believed to be more transparent and accountable than the ECB. Transparency brings credibility, which should reduce inflationary expectations. The BOE publishes monthly minutes of its meetings, the ECB does not. Details of how members voted are kept secret by the ECB whilst they are made public in UK. However, the ECB argues that through the release of ECB monthly bulletins and its president's speeches, the ECB is accountable enough.

Question

3. Contrast the monetary policy-making process of the European Central Bank with that of the Bank of England.

● ● Knowledge and Application: Gordon Brown's five economic tests

The position of the UK government is that it is willing to join the single currency but only when membership is in the UK's economic interests. Therefore in 1997 Gordon Brown devised the five economic tests in order to determine whether the UK is ready for the single currency. The five tests as summarised by HM Treasury, are:

(i) **Cyclical convergence**: are business cycles and economic structures compatible so that we and others could live comfortably with euro interest rates on a permanent basis? This test includes the housing market, where there are significant differences between the UK and the Eurozone. These include the fact that in Europe mortgage rates are linked to long term rather than short-term interest rates, and also that a higher percentage of households own their own home in the UK compared to the EU.

(ii) **Flexibility**: if problems emerge (e.g. asymmetric shocks) is there sufficient flexibility to deal with them?

(iii) **Inward investment**: would joining EMU create better conditions for firms making long-term decisions to invest in Britain?

(iv) **The impact on the financial sector**: what impact would entry into EMU have on the competitive position of the UK's financial services industry, particularly the City's wholesale markets?

(v) **The effect on growth and employment**: will joining EMU promote higher growth, stability and a lasting increase in jobs?

● Evaluation of the UK's readiness to join the euro

A comprehensive assessment of the five tests by the government in 2003 concluded that only one out of the five tests, the financial services test, had been passed. The convergence and flexibility criteria had definitely not been met, while the wording of the conclusions of the other two tests was ambiguous, but both were far from a clear 'yes'. However, the wording of many of the tests is extremely vague, and the impact of EMU on many of the above factors is difficult to gauge. This has prompted critics to say that the government could easily fudge the issue. These critics feel the government could claim that all of the economic tests had been passed as soon as it has decided that it is politically viable to join, for example, if public opinion moves in favour of EMU. The most important test, and the one most difficult to fudge, is arguably the cyclical convergence test. Although the UK business cycle is more synchronised with that of the Eurozone now compared to 1997, the government has decided that they are still not sufficiently converged. Despite the recession and the decline in the value of the pound compared to the euro, in 2009 the issue of UK membership of the single currency once again seems to have been put on the 'back-burner'.

Question

4. Examine the costs and benefits to the UK economy of joining the euro.

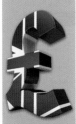

● Knowledge: EU enlargement and the immigration issue

The criteria for the 12 new countries that have joined the EU since 2004 included a functioning market economy, institutional stability, democracy and a willingness for political, economic and monetary union.

● Analysis: The benefits of enlargement

In theory, the same benefits from specialisation and trade outlined above should be reaped as the Single European Market expands and UK businesses have the opportunity to access the largest free trade and investment area in the world:

(i)   Businesses should benefit from economies of scale. Growth in many of the new countries has been impressive recently, particularly Estonia, Latvia and Lithuania. Having said this, the relatively low per capita income of the new members may limit the amount of effective demand, at least initially.

(ii) UK consumers should be able to buy a wider range of goods and services and the effects of competition should bring prices down.

(iii) The law of comparative advantage should be able to work rather well as its function depends on differences between the economic structure of different countries. The new members have a higher share of economic activity devoted to primary production and manufacturing than the EU15, so there should be plenty of scope for gains from trade. The DTI estimated that EU enlargement should increase UK GDP by £1.75 billion, while the Centre for Economic Policy Research suggests 300,000 jobs will be created in the UK.

Table 11.4: EU accession countries, selected indicators

Country	Population (million, 2006)	GDP/capita (% EU average 2006)	Unemployment Rate (% May 2007)	Inflation (% CPI May 2007)
Bulgaria	7.72	N/A	7.2	4.5
Cyprus	0.77	80	4.1	1.9
Czech Republic	10.25	48	5.7	2.4
Estonia	1.34	43	5.2	5.9
Hungary	10.08	39	5.7	8.4
Latvia	2.29	32	5.8	7.8
Lithuania	3.40	31	4.9	5.0
Malta	0.44	49	6.5	-1.0
Poland	38.16	31	10.5	2.3
Romania	21.61	N/A	7.3	3.9
Slovak Republic	5.39	37	10.8	1.5
Slovenia	2.00	64	5.1	3.1
EU 27	**492.96**	**100**	**7.0**	**2.1**

Source: Eurostat

There are at least two other potential effects of EU enlargement, however.

(i)   There will have to be a substantial transfer of resources from the original EU15 to the new members. This has already happened to some extent in the run up to enlargement: under the PHARE process money has been given to accession countries for institutional building and investment.[5] The main problem here, however, is that the new members are much more dependent on agriculture than the EU15 and will therefore demand larger subsidies from farming. This has contributed to substantial reform of the Common Agricultural Policy, including a freezing of the CAP budget, and a move away

---

5. A programme financed by the EU to assist accession countries before joining the EU. PHARE stood for 'Poland and Hungary: Assistance for Restructuring their Economies'.

Harvest in Poland: New EU members are more dependent on agriculture and need larger subsidies.

from price support towards income support for farmers. There will be costs here not just of reforming the CAP but also the cost to EU15 farmers of losing price support. EU regional policy will also need to be reformed as under the current system those with a GDP level of less than 75% of the EU average receive substantial monetary benefits. Most of the new members will qualify for these monetary benefits under the existing system.

(ii) A large inflow of Eastern European migrant workers to the EU15, including the UK. In the two years after the 2004 accession, nearly 600,000 workers came from Eastern Europe to work in the UK, such as Polish plumbers! The UK was one of only three countries to have an 'open door' policy to immigrant workers, a policy it has now rescinded for Romanian and Bulgarian migrants in 2007. Unemployment in some of the new member states, such as Poland, is relatively high, especially youth unemployment, and it was to be expected that countries like the UK, with relatively lax immigration policies, would receive a large influx of migrants.

● Evaluation: The net advantages to the UK of an influx of migrant workers

(i) Migrant workers raise the UK working population, and produce output, raising the productive potential of the economy.

(ii) The workers pay taxes and national insurance contributions, improving the government's financial position. With our 'pay as you go' pension system, this factor is particularly significant.

(iii) The rise in the labour supply holds down wages and therefore helps the Bank of England to control inflation.

The potential macroeconomic effects, therefore, would appear to be positive. However:

(i) Migrant workers may put a strain on public services, such as schooling and welfare benefits.

(ii) They may reduce wages and living standards for UK workers with which they are competing as they are often prepared to work for a lower wage in industries such as construction.

(ii) It is argued that there should be more assistance for economically inactive UK workers to do the jobs

that the migrant workers are doing. Stories that many immigrants have not looked for work and lived off benefits have been common in the British press, although official statistics indicate that these reports have been greatly exaggerated.

(iv) Within the SEM, family and social ties, language barriers and differences in job qualifications will limit the degree of immigration possible.

(v) There may be some relocation by UK firms to the new member states. However, this will not significantly affect UK unemployment any more than the outsourcing of call centres has done. By the same token, immigration should not cause unemployment in the UK: rather, it will alleviate labour shortages in jobs which UK workers don't want to do, such as manual labour.

On 16 October 2007, two separate studies from the Home Office appeared to confirm the views of both sides discussed above. One said that immigrants contribute £6 billion to the UK economy and are harder working than the native population. The other report warned of the strain that migrants are putting on housing, health and policing in many areas of the UK. The debate, both political and economic, will undoubtedly run and run on this most emotive of subjects.

● Knowledge: The Common Agricultural Policy (CAP)

We turn finally to consider agriculture in the EU. The initial aims of the CAP were as follows:

- To increase farm productivity.
- To guarantee EU food supplies.
- To stabilise agricultural markets.
- Reasonable prices for consumers.
- A fair standard of living for EU farmers.

● Application: Regulated trade

Under the CAP, EU farmers are guaranteed a target price for their products sold on EU markets which is above the market equilibrium. The EU buys up the excess supply at this price level: this is known as **intervention buying**. Export subsidies provide the incentive for traders to buy agricultural goods at a high price and sell them on world markets at lower prices. The CAP has enabled the EU to become self sufficient in food, and it could be argued that it helps the environment, since farmers look after the countryside and preserve it for future generations. It also helps sustain the rural parts of the EU economy.

● Analysis: Does the CAP distort trade?

The CAP has been heavily criticised, for the following reasons:

- **Higher consumer prices**: It is estimated that British households pay an extra £832 a year in grocery bills because of the CAP, reducing consumer welfare.

- **Higher cost to the taxpayer**: The CAP cost £30 billion in 2006.

- **Distortion of world trade**: This arises because surpluses are sold on overseas markets at subsidised rates. Thousands of tonnes of subsidised exports are dumped in Africa every year, driving local producers of products such as sugar, wheat, milk and chicken out of the market. Storing surpluses involves high costs of storage.

- **Overintensive farming**: CAP subsidies cause negative externalities such as damage to farm land.

- **Equity issues**: Protectionist policies lead to lop-sided distribution of benefits. 20% of farmers get 80% of the support! Also some countries, such as UK, are big net contributors, while France is a big net recipient. The UK is a net contributor due to its small and relatively efficient farming sector.

The McSharry reforms of 1992 led to cuts in the intervention prices and the introduction of a set-aside scheme, in which farmers were paid to let land lie fallow, so that supply fell without a loss in farmers' earnings. Since 1992, the trend has been to move away from a system of price support to a system of income support for EU farmers. Further reform came in 2000 under Agenda 2000. Intervention prices were cut further and new rural development schemes funded farmers for activities other than farming. The Rural Development Policy pays farmers to stimulate investment in farm business, forestry, improve training for young farmers and provide early retirement schemes for agricultural workers.

In 2003, the CAP received its biggest change yet under the Fischler reforms. Most countries have now moved towards a system of annual single farm payments. Farmers need to meet animal welfare, environmental, food hygiene and health and safety standards in order to qualify for payments. Crucially, the subsidies are now paid not for output of crops but for a number of environmental schemes and rural development schemes. Farmers now have to plan output on the basis of market prices. Subsidies to the largest farms are being gradually reduced. Intervention prices have been cut for sugar, milk and butter. The idea is that market forces will now play a greater role in EU agriculture and the environmental schemes will help to correct for any externalities that may arise.

The main reason why the CAP has been reformed recently is because of complaints made to the World Trade Organisation (WTO) from the United States and from developing countries. Not only did they argue against the EU's dumping policy, they also complained that the Common External Tariff restricted access to EU markets. In 2005, the EU sugar regime was ruled illegal by the World Trade Organisation due to the dumping of too much subsidised sugar in developing countries (dumping means when surplus goods are sold abroad at a price below average cost).

Spending on the CAP as a percentage of the EU Budget is being gradually reduced. This was always inevitable given that the accession of the CEEC countries in 2004 increased the number of EU farmers by 70%! In 2007, the EU planned to spend 34% of the EU Budget on direct aids and market measures in agriculture, compared to nearly 70% in the early 1980s.

Question

5. Explain the economic consequences of the CAP.